Rock Hits
for Ukulele

Alfred Music Publishing Co., Inc.

Los Angeles

Contributing Editor: *Andrew DuBrock*

Recordings: *Chauncey Gardiner Combo, featuring Armando Strange on ukulele, Erick Lynen on vocals, and guest Gayle Giese on vocals for "Tonight You Belong to Me"*

Cover Photo: *Chocolate Heart Mango Concert Classic Ukulele courtesy of Gordon and Char Mayer, of Mya-Moe Ukuleles*

Contents

Reviewing the Basics

Songs

Appendixes

Artist Index

Introduction

We all play music for pretty much the same reason—to play our favorite songs. It's so easy to get caught up in mastering technique, learning to read music, or understanding music theory, that we can spend hours at the instrument and still not have a good song to play. Note reading, technique, and theory are all great tools—but that's all they are. The focus of this book is to get you playing your favorite songs now! Playing your favorite songs is the single most important musical learning experience you can have. All the songs in this book use related chords, scales, techniques, and other elements, so as you learn your favorite songs, you are actually learning the skills you need to play other favorites as well.

Everything is included to help you play every song. First, there is a review of the basics, like holding the ukulele and reading music and TAB. Every song is then presented with a short lesson that explores the tricks to making it easy to play. All the music is shown in standard music notation, TAB, and ukulele chords so you can choose which is best for you. At the back of the book, there is a huge chord dictionary to help you play even more songs from sheet music and other books.

Most important are the recordings on the included CDs. Musicians learn by listening and imitating—the way a child learns to speak. Our included recordings allow you to learn in the most natural way possible—by listening and imitating. If you use the CDs in your CD player, you can hear ukulele versions of all the songs in the book. If you use the CDs in your computer and access the TNT software included on the discs, you can hear three versions of each song: the full-performance ukulele recording, a version without vocals so you can hear the ukulele parts more clearly, and a version without ukulele so you can play along with the band. Listen to them often, and keep them handy as you learn each song. It's not important that you master every aspect of every song. You can focus on the parts that grab your attention the most—a lick you like, the melody, the chords, anything you *want* to play. As you gain experience, technique, and knowledge, putting the pieces together and learning the complete songs will get easier and easier. Also, the TNT software lets you loop sections for practice, slow tracks down or speed them up without changing the pitch, and even change the key. With so many tools at your disposal, you'll be able to nail any song you want in no time.

Be sure to check out the other books in this series to see if there are other favorites you'd like to learn. If you want more information on playing music, reading music, or even writing your own music, there are lots of other *Complete Idiot's Guides* to help you along.

Now tune your ukulele, crank up your recordings, and dig in.

How to Use This Book

Some people approach learning an instrument by isolating all the technical skills, and, through years of study and practice, develop a command of those skills and tools. Others learn by having a friend show them a simple song, and then proceed to learn on a song-by-song basis. Some combination of the two methods is probably the best, but you should always spend a good portion of your music time learning songs that you would really love to perform for your friends and family—or for yourself.

In this book, each song is written in full music notation and TAB (tablature). Reading music is a skill acquired through diligent practice, and it has many benefits. But TAB offers a quick way of knowing what to play without having to be an accomplished music reader. We believe that providing TAB in conjunction with standard music notation is the ideal way to get you up and playing right away. Ukulele chord grids indicate chord fingerings for strumming and fingerpicking accompaniment parts.

Start by picking a song you really want to play. Then listen carefully to the provided recording (and the original version). Music is an aural art, so always have the sound of the song clearly in your head before you attempt to learn to play it on the ukulele.

Read through the lesson that precedes each song and practice the music examples before attempting to play the whole song. Each lesson is broken into various sections. We've also included other info along the way to point out things that are particularly important, interesting, or helpful.

The disc and track number of the song on the included CDs. The TNT software allows access to play-along, looping, and tempo options. See the TNT instructions below.

 A brief introduction to the song.

 The main body of the lesson, with tips, pointers, excerpts, examples, and other helpful information.

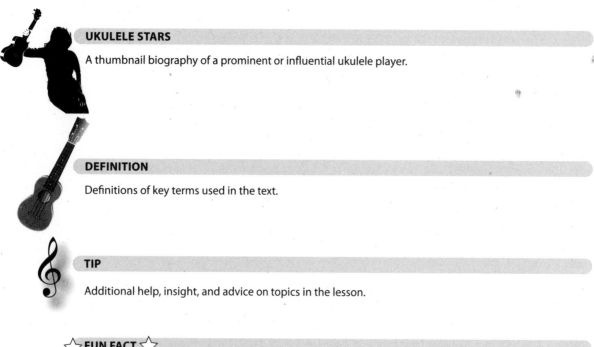

UKULELE STARS

A thumbnail biography of a prominent or influential ukulele player.

DEFINITION

Definitions of key terms used in the text.

TIP

Additional help, insight, and advice on topics in the lesson.

☆ **FUN FACT** ☆

Interesting trivia about an artist or the song.

If you want to know more about chords, be sure to read Appendix A. It will teach you about the different kinds of chords, how they are constructed, and what the symbols mean.

Appendix B is a diagram of the ukulele fretboard, showing every note on every string up to the 12th fret.

Appendix C is a huge chord dictionary with 192 chords to help you play other songs from sheet music or at jam sessions.

Finally, we've provided a glossary in Appendix D that covers all the musical terms used throughout this book.

About the TNT Tone 'N' Tempo Changer Software

For complete instructions, see the *TnT ReadMe.pdf* file on your enhanced CDs.

Windows users: insert a CD into your computer, double-click on My Computer, right-click on your CD drive icon, and select Explore to locate the file.

Mac users: insert a CD into your computer and double-click on the CD icon on your desktop to locate the file.

Trademarks

Reviewing the Basics

Getting to Know Your Ukulele

You may or may not be able to name all the parts of your ukulele, and you may or may not need to. If you ever get into a conversation with another ukulele player, however, it will probably go better if you know what is being referred to as "the nut" or "the bridge."

The Parts of the Ukulele

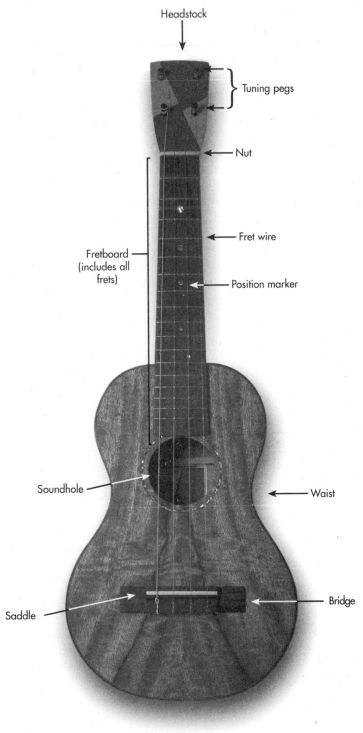

Headstock

Tuning pegs

Nut

Fret wire

Fretboard
(includes all
frets)

Position marker

Soundhole

Waist

Saddle

Bridge

Ukulele Types

Soprano: For most people, this is what first comes to mind when talking about ukulele. The soprano is the smallest of the four ukulele types, and is 13 inches in scale (the distance from the nut to the bridge). For comparison, a guitar typically has a 25 inch scale. The soprano has a very bright tone and is often given to novices interested in learning the ukulele, however, due to its very small size, it can be difficult to hold onto and even harder for people with large hands. The soprano is tuned to standard ukulele tuning: G'–C'–E'–A' (the prime symbol ['] means the note is in the octave above middle C).

Concert: The concert ukulele is larger than the soprano, with a scale length of 15 inches. The concert uke also has a fuller sound than the soprano and is easier to play, especially for larger hands. The concert uke can be tuned exactly like the soprano or with the G string tuned one octave lower. For a complete explanation of standard and Low G tunings, see Tuning Your Ukulele, starting on page 5.

Tenor: The tenor is the second largest ukulele type and is 17 inches in scale. While the tenor is usually tuned like both the soprano and concert ukes (G'–C'–E'–A'), it has a much fuller sound. Some tenor ukes have six strings (tuned like a high-pitched guitar) or even eight (tuned to standard ukulele tuning but with each string doubled for a mandolin-like sound).

Baritone: This is the largest of the ukuleles, featuring a 19-inch scale length. It resembles a small guitar, and is usually tuned like the top four strings of a guitar (D–G–B–E'). The baritone uke has the deepest tone and is usually used to provide the bass range that's missing in the other ukuleles.

Type	Scale	Total Length	Tuning*
Soprano	13 inches	21 inches	G'–C'–E'–A'
Concert	15 inches	23 inches	G'–C'–E'–A' or G–C'–E'–A'
Tenor	17 inches	26 inches	G'–C'–E'–A' or G–C'–E'–A'
Baritone	19 inches	30 inches	D–G–B–E'

*The prime symbol (') means the note is in the octave above middle C.

How to Hold Your Ukulele

Below are two typical ways of holding your ukulele. Pick the one that is most comfortable for you.

Sitting.

Standing with strap.

Using Your Right Hand

Sometimes your right hand will play individual notes on a single string, and sometimes it will play chords using many strings. To *strum* means to play several strings by brushing quickly across them, usually with your fingers but sometimes with a pick. This is the most common way of playing a chord.

Strumming with Your Fingers

First, decide if you feel more comfortable strumming with the side of your thumb or with the nail of your fingers.

On a *down-stroke*, strum from the string closest to the ceiling to the string closest to the floor. Move mostly your wrist, not just your arm. For an *up-stroke*, strum from the string closest to the floor to the string closest to the ceiling.

TIP

Strumming is done mostly from the wrist, not the arm. Use as little motion as possible. Start as close to the string as you can, and never let your hand move past the edge of the ukulele.

Strumming with the thumb.

Strumming with the fingers.

Strumming with a Pick

Strumming with a pick is often too much for the nylon strings of a ukulele, so uke players most often strum with their fingers. For the rare instances that you do want to use a pick, hold it between your thumb and index finger. Hold the pick firmly, but don't squeeze too hard. The strumming motion is the same when using the pick as it is with the thumb or fingers.

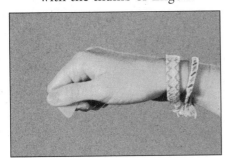

Holding the pick.

Starting near the 4th string.

Finishing near the 1st string.

Using Your Left Hand

Your left hand needs to be relaxed when you play. It's also important to keep your fingernails neat and trim so that your fingers will curve in just the right way, otherwise you'll hear lots of buzzing and muffling.

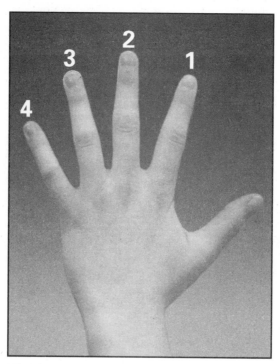

The left-hand finger numbers.

Proper Left-Hand Position

Your left-hand fingers will work best when your hand is correctly shaped and positioned. Place your hand so your thumb rests comfortably in the middle of the back of the neck and your wrist is away from the fretboard. Your fingers should be perpendicular to the fretboard.

Front view.

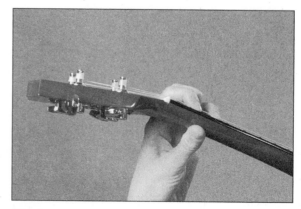

Top view.

Placing a Finger on a String

When you press a string with a left-hand finger, make sure you press firmly with the tip of your finger and as close to the fret wire as you can without actually being right on it. This will create a clean, bright tone. If your finger is too far from the fret wire, the note will buzz. If it is on top of the fret wire, you'll get a muffled, unclear sound. Also, make sure your finger stays clear of neighboring strings.

Right! The finger is close to the fret wire.

Wrong! The finger is too far from the fret wire.

Wrong! The finger is on top of the fret wire.

Tuning Your Ukulele

Every musician knows the agony of hearing an instrument that is not in tune. Always be sure to tune your ukulele every time you play, and check the tuning every now and then between songs.

About the Tuning Pegs

First, make sure your strings are wound properly around the tuning pegs. They should go from the inside to the outside as shown in the illustration. Turning a tuning peg clockwise makes the pitch lower, and turning a tuning peg counter-clockwise makes the pitch higher. Be sure not to tune the strings too high, or you run the risk of breaking them.

TIP

Always remember that the string closest to the floor is the *1st* string. The string closest to the ceiling is the *4th* string.

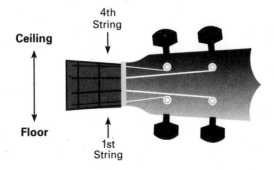

Tuning Using the Included CDs

If you pop one of the included discs into your CD player, you'll notice that the first track is a tuning track. For your convenience, both CDs have the tuning track.

The first note plucked is the 1st string, and the track continues through the 2nd, 3rd, and 4th strings. So one by one, make sure the pitches of the strings on your ukulele match the notes you hear on the tuning track. Just adjust your tuning pegs accordingly. It may be difficult at first, but with practice and lots of attentive listening, it'll come naturally.

Standard ukulele tuning is G–C–E–A, with the G note on the "lowest" string actually sounding higher in pitch than the next two strings. This kind of tuning is called *reentrant tuning*—a tuning in which the notes are not ordered from the lowest to highest pitch. A variation of standard uke tuning is *Low G tuning*. In Low G, the G string is lowered one octave. This tuning sounds best when you use a thicker G string.

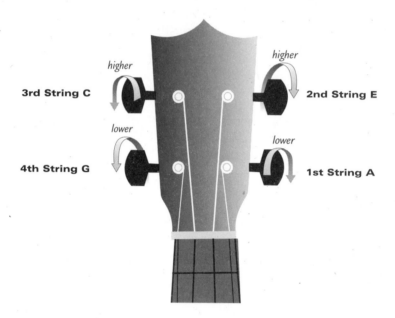

Tuning the Ukulele to Itself

The day will surely come when your ukulele is out of tune but you don't have your trusty play-along CDs with tuning tracks. If your 3rd string is in tune, you can tune the rest of the strings using the ukulele by itself. The easiest way to tune the 3rd string is with a piano. If you don't have a piano available, consider buying an electronic tuner or pitch pipe. There are many types available, and a salesperson at your local music store can help you decide which is best for you.

If you have access to a piano, tune the 3rd string to the note C above middle C.

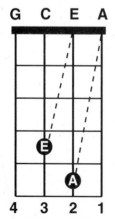 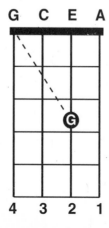

To tune the rest of the strings, follow this sequence:

- Tune the open 2nd string (E) to the note at the 4th fret of the 3rd string.

- Tune the open 1st string (A) to the note at the 5th fret of the 2nd string.

- Tune the open 4th string (G) to the note at the 3rd fret of the 2nd string.

The Basics of Music Notation

Standard music notation contains a plethora of musical information. If you don't already read notation, you will probably benefit from studying the following fundamental concepts. Understanding even a little about reading notation can help you create a performance that is true to the original.

Notes

Notes are used to indicate musical sounds. Some notes are held long and others are short.

Note Values		
whole note	**o**	4 beats
half note	♩	2 beats
quarter note	♩	1 beat
eighth note	♪	½ beat
sixteenth note	♬	¼ beat

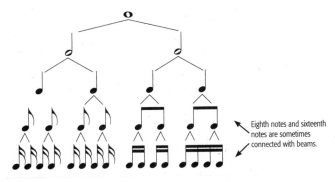

Eighth notes and sixteenth notes are sometimes connected with beams.

Relative note values.

When a *dot* follows a note, the length of the note is longer by one half of the note's original length.

Dotted Note Values		
dotted half note	♩.	3 beats
dotted quarter note	♩.	1 ½ beats
dotted eighth note	♪.	¾ beat

A *triplet* is a group of three notes played in the time of two. Triplets are identified by a small numeral "3" over the note group.

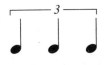

Quarter-note triplet.

Rests

Rests are used to indicate musical silence.

Rest Values		
whole rest	▬	4 beats
half rest	▬	2 beats
quarter rest	𝄽	1 beat
eighth rest	𝄾	½ beat
sixteenth rest	𝄿	¼ beat

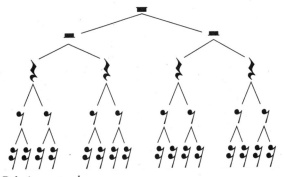

Relative rest values.

The Staff

Music is written on a *staff* made up of five lines and four spaces, numbered from the bottom up. Each line and space is designated as a different pitch.

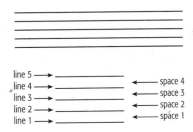

line 5 → ___ ← space 4
line 4 → ___ ← space 3
line 3 → ___ ← space 2
line 2 → ___ ← space 1
line 1 → ___

The staff is divided into equal units of time called *measures* or *bars*.

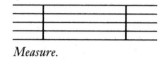

Measure.

A *bar line* indicates where one measure ends and another begins.

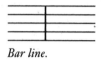

Bar line.

A *double bar line*, made of one thin line and one thick line, shows the end of a piece of music.

Double bar line.

Notes on the Staff

Notes are named using the first seven letters of the alphabet (A B C D E F G). The higher a note is on the staff, the higher its pitch.

E F G A B C D E F

The *treble clef*, also called the *G clef*, is the curly symbol you see at the beginning of each staff. The treble clef designates the second line of the staff as the note G.

Here are the notes on the lines of the treble staff. An easy way to remember them is with the phrase "Every Good Boy Does Fine."

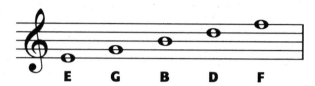

E G B D F

Notes on the lines.

Here are the notes on the spaces. They are easy to remember because they spell the word FACE.

F A C E

Notes on the spaces.

The staff can be extended to include even higher or lower notes by using *ledger lines*. You can think of ledger lines as small pieces of additional staff lines and spaces. The C note in the middle is the open C string—the lowest note on your ukulele.

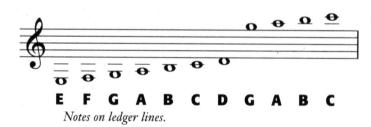

E F G A B C D G A B C

Notes on ledger lines.

Accidentals

An *accidental* raises or lowers the sound of a note. A *sharp* ♯ raises a note one *half step*, which is the distance from one fret to another. A *flat* ♭ lowers a note one half step. A *natural* ♮ cancels a sharp or a flat. An accidental remains in effect until the end of the measure, so if the same note has to be played flat or sharp again, only the first one will have the accidental. See the Ukulele Fingerboard Chart on page 163 for all the flat and sharp notes on the ukulele up to the 12th fret.

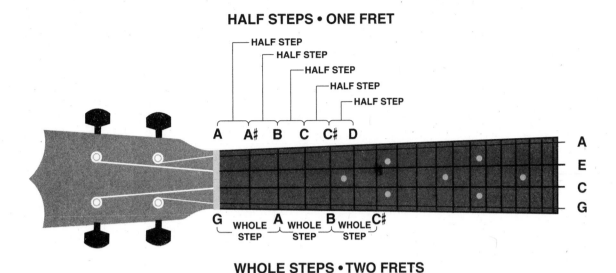

Key Signatures

Sometimes certain notes need to be played sharp or flat throughout an entire song. In this case, it's easier to put the sharps or flats in the *key signature* instead of putting an accidental on each individual note. If you see sharps or flats at the beginning of a staff just after the treble clef, that means to play those notes sharp or flat throughout the music. The key signature can change within a song as well, so be sure to keep an eye out. Below are two examples of key signatures.

Play each F, C, and G as F♯, C♯, and G♯.

Play each B and E as B♭ and E♭.

Time Signatures

The *time signature* is a symbol resembling a fraction that appears at the beginning of the music. The top number tells you how many beats are in each measure, and the bottom number tells you what kind of note gets one beat. Most songs have the same number of beats in every measure, but the time signature can also change within a song. It's important to notice each time signature and count correctly, otherwise you could end up getting ahead in the song or falling behind.

$\frac{4}{4}$ Time

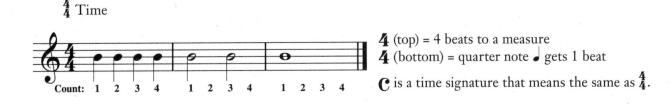

4 (top) = 4 beats to a measure

4 (bottom) = quarter note ♩ gets 1 beat

𝄴 is a time signature that means the same as $\frac{4}{4}$.

3 = 3 beats to a measure
4 = quarter note ♩ gets 1 beat

6 = 6 beats to a measure
8 = eighth note ♪ gets 1 beat

9 = 9 beats to a measure
8 = eighth note ♪ gets 1 beat

12 = 12 beats to a measure
8 = eighth note ♪ gets 1 beat

TIP

A whole rest always means rest for a whole measure. So in ¾ the rest is three beats, in 6/8 it is six beats, and so on.

Ties

A *tie* is a curved line that joins two or more notes of the same pitch, which tells you to play them as one continuous note. Instead of playing the second note, continue to hold for the combined note value. Ties make it possible to write notes that last longer than one measure, or notes with unusual values.

Hold B for five beats.

The Fermata

A *fermata* ⌢ over a note means to pause, holding for about twice as long as usual.

Pause on notes with a fermata.

Repeat Signs

Most songs don't start and then ramble on in one continuous stream of thought to the end. They are constructed with sections, such as verses and choruses, that are repeated in some organized pattern. To avoid having to go through pages and pages of duplicate music, several different types of *repeat signs* are used to show what to play over again. Repeat signs act as a kind of roadmap, telling you when to go back and where to go next, navigating you through the song.

Repeat Dots

The simplest repeat sign is simply two dots on the inside of a double bar. It means to go back to the beginning and play the music over again.

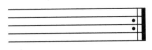

Go back and play again.

When just a section of music is to be repeated, an opposite repeat sign at the beginning of the section tells you to repeat everything in between.

Repeat everything between facing repeat signs.

1st and 2nd Endings

When a section is repeated but the ending needs to be different, the *1st ending* shows what to play the first time, and the *2nd ending* shows what to play the second time. Play the 1st ending, repeat, then skip the 1st ending and play the 2nd ending.

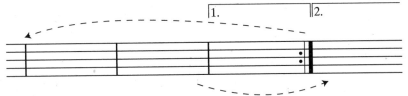

Play the 1st ending, repeat, then skip to the 2nd ending.

Other Repeat Signs

D.C. al Fine	Repeat from the beginning and end at ***Fine***.
D.C. al Coda	Repeat from the beginning and play to the coda sign ⊕, then skip to the ***Coda*** and play to the end.
D.S. al Fine	Repeat from the sign 𝄋 and end at ***Fine***.
D.S. al Coda	Repeat from the sign 𝄋 and play to the coda sign ⊕, then skip to the ***Coda*** and play to the end.

Reading Ukulele Tablature (TAB)

Tablature, or *TAB* for short, is a graphic representation of the four strings of the ukulele. Although standard notation tells you which notes and rhythms to play, the TAB staff tells you quickly where to finger each note on the ukulele. The bottom line of the TAB staff represents the 4th string, and the top line is the 1st string. Notes and chords are indicated by the placement of fret numbers on each string.

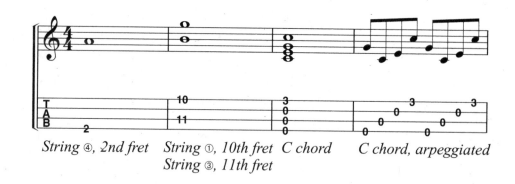

String ④, 2nd fret   String ①, 10th fret   C chord   C chord, arpeggiated
                      String ③, 11th fret

The following are examples of various ukulele techniques you might come across in the notation of the songs. Unless otherwise indicated, the left hand does the work for these.

Articulations

Hammer-on: Play the lower note, then "hammer" your left-hand finger onto the string to sound the higher note. Only the first note is plucked.

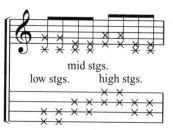

Muted strings: A percussive sound is produced by striking the strings with the right hand while laying the fret hand across them.

Pull-off: Play the higher note with your first finger already in position on the lower note. Pull your finger off the first note with a strong downward motion that plucks the string, sounding the lower note.

Palm mute: The notes are muted (muffled) by placing the palm of the right hand lightly on the strings, just in front of the bridge.

Legato slide: Play the first note, and with continued pressure applied to the string, slide up or down to the second note. The diagonal line shows that it is a slide and not a hammer-on or a pull-off.

Picking Direction

Down-strokes and up-strokes: The down-stroke is indicated with this symbol ⊓, and the up-stroke is indicated with this one ∨.

Songs

Another Brick in the Wall (Part II)

Key Thoughts

Progressive rock heroes Pink Floyd had already mastered the concept album with *Dark Side of the Moon* and *Wish You Were Here*. But *The Wall* is arguably even more iconic than those earlier albums—certainly in scope, as it takes two complete records to run its course. Though conceived as a concept album, the record had plenty of punch on the singles charts due to the standout track "Another Brick in the Wall (Part II)," which topped the Billboard Hot 100. Along with its chart success, the album received a Grammy in 1980 for Best Engineered Recording. Originally written as a rock opera, *The Wall* was also released as a musical film three years later.

Take Note

Many songs use eighth notes in their strum patterns, but "Another Brick in the Wall (Part II)" uses sixteenth notes as its foundation. This means there are many more strums in each measure, and all of those notes can look intimidating. But if you slow things down and count along, you can master even the most difficult-looking rhythms. Break each beat into sixteenth-note subdivisions by saying "1-e-&-a, 2-e-&-a, 3-e-&-a, 4-e-&-a," as shown in the following example. Move your hand in a constant down-and-up motion along with your counting, making sure your hand is moving down on "1." Keep strumming with your finger in the air just in front of your ukulele strings, and connect with the strings only on beats that have a strum notated. This type of strumming, often called *pendulum strumming*, might make it easier for you to understand the rhythmic pattern. Once you have the pattern down, you probably won't need to move your hand up and down as much between strums.

Verse:

At measure 13, the strum pattern switches to steady sixteenth notes before a fairly challenging chordal lick in measure 19. This lick moves by quickly, but if you use the suggested fret-hand fingerings, it'll probably be easier for you to move between chords. This means that you'll need to barre the high Dm chord with your ring finger, leaving your index and middle fingers handy to grab the C chord that comes next. After moving between these chords a few times, slide down the neck to play the G and F chords. Slow it down and count along if you need to, just as we did with the strum pattern. And if you want to play through the song before mastering the lick, you can leave the riff out and things will still sound fine; instead, just play the root-position Dm chord, and strum either the opening strum pattern or the rhythms of the lick. Also, remember that you can always use the TNT software on the included CDs to slow everything down and loop the lick for repeated practice.

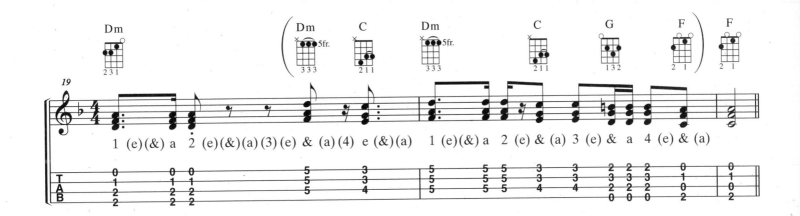

☆ **FUN FACT** ☆

There are many different versions of "Another Brick in the Wall (Part II)." The album version (on which this ukulele rendition is based) immediately jumps into the verse at the tail-end of a scream from the previous song, and ends with jabbering dialog, sounds of a playground, and a ringing phone. The single version has a short intro—with the guitar playing the first strum pattern—then fades out near the end of the guitar solo. Hybrid versions of these two also exist, along with completely different takes featuring such variations as a tapped guitar part, slap bass, and organ solo.

Another Brick in the Wall (Part II)

Words and Music by
ROGER WATERS

Moderately ♩ = 104

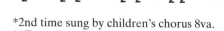

*2nd time sung by children's chorus 8va.
**Tacet first two measures on repeat.

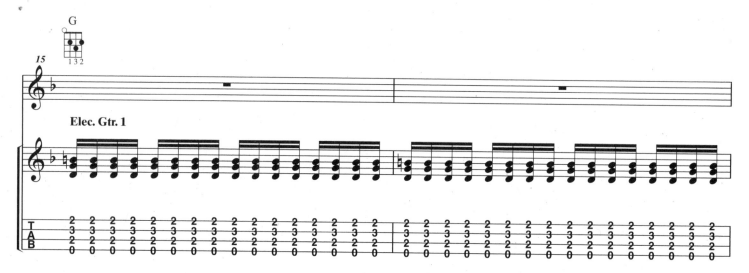

Boulevard of Broken Dreams

In 2004, Green Day was dangerously close to becoming a forgotten band. Their popularity was declining, they hadn't released a record in four years, and their previous album, *Warning*, had been much less successful than their earlier records. But that year, Green Day released one of their strongest and most successful records. *American Idiot* debuted at No. 1 on the Billboard 200 album chart, and the record acquired two Grammys—one in 2004 for Best Rock Album, and one in 2005 for "Boulevard of Broken Dreams" as Record of the Year.

"Boulevard of Broken Dreams" features the static chord progression Fm–A♭–E♭–B♭ throughout the intro and verses. The only thing that changes is the strumming pattern. When a progression repeats as long as this, it's always a good idea to find the most efficient way to finger the chords in conjunction with each other. One way to streamline things is to barre the top three strings with your index finger for the Fm chord. That way, you only need to lift your pinky finger off of the 3rd string to play the A♭ chord.

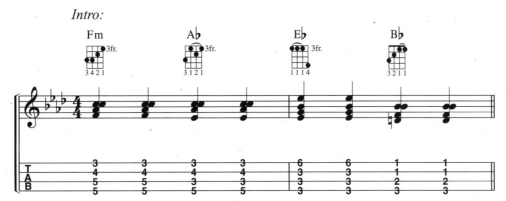

As the verse begins, the strumming pattern gets a little busier, incorporating *scratch rhythm* to propel things forward. Indicated by slashed "x" noteheads, scratch rhythm requires you to mute the strings with your fretting hand while strumming through for a "chukka" sound. (For more on scratch rhythm, see the lesson for "Big Yellow Taxi.") Of course, the best way to get a sense for how something sounds is to *listen*, so cue up the audio, and remember that with the TNT software you can loop and slow down sections.

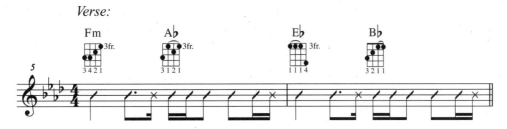

 **FUN FACT**

Green Day's *American Idiot* and *21st Century Breakdown* were both concept albums. *American Idiot* was adapted into a musical and had such a successful debut at the Berkeley Repertory Theatre in California that it moved on to Broadway in early 2010.

Boulevard of Broken Dreams

Words by BILLIE JOE
Music by GREEN DAY

Chorus:

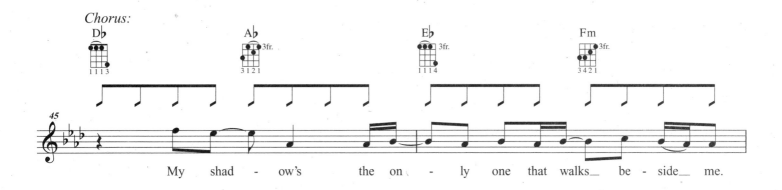

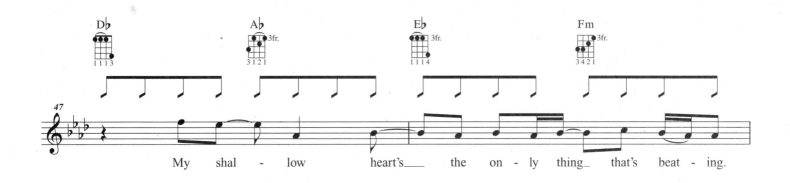

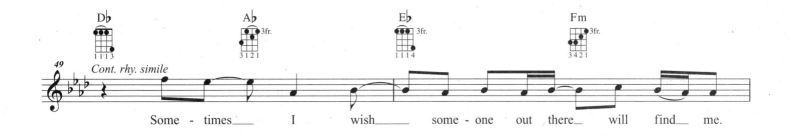

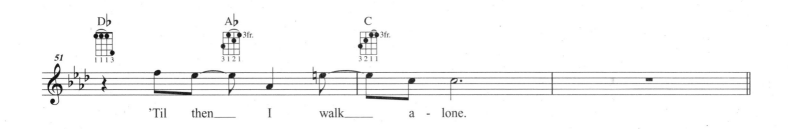

Outro: *Play 4 times*

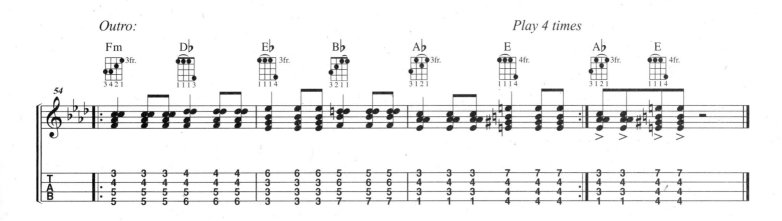

Bad to the Bone

George Thorogood had his major-label debut in 1982 with *Bad to the Bone*, and the album's title track became his signature song. Over the past three decades, the song has become so synonymous with the bad-boy image that it's appeared in many films, TV shows, and video games.

Take Note

For "Bad to the Bone," George Thorogood uses a guitar tuned to *Open G tuning* and plays the licks with a slide. Open tunings are great for slides—all you have to do is lay the slide across the strings at any fret and you'll have a chord (see the definition for *altered* and *open tunings*). Because the sound of this song is so tied to the tuning and slide, the arrangement has been adapted to a ukulele in Open G tuning. To get your ukulele in tune, start by tuning your 1st string down to G. That's the same note that your 4th string is already tuned to, so you can simply match your 1st string to your 4th string. Then, tune your 2nd string down so that when you play the note at the 5th fret of the 2nd string, it matches the open 1st string. If done correctly, this will make your open 2nd string a D. Finally, tune your 3rd string down so that when you hold the 3rd fret of the 3rd string, the note matches the open 2nd string (after the 2nd string has been tuned down). This will make your open 3rd string a B note.

DEFINITION

When you tune your ukulele's strings to anything other than standard tuning, you're in an **altered tuning**. There are countless altered tunings for the guitar, and many ukulele players have adapted these to the uke. Tuning to the notes of any major or minor chord puts you in an **open tuning**. "Bad to the Bone" is in an open tuning; since it's tuned to a G chord, it's called **Open G tuning**.

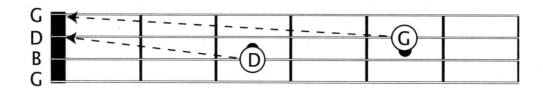

Once you're in the correct tuning, place the slide on your ring or pinky finger. This leaves your other fingers available to fret notes to the left of the slide. On the original recording, the barred chords at the 5th and 12th frets are played with the slide, while single-note lines and the barred chords at the 3rd fret are mostly played with the other fingers.

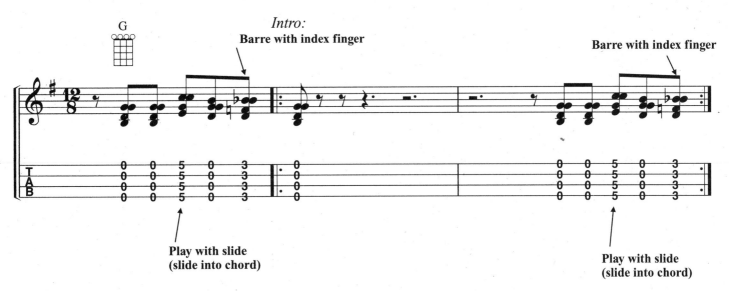

Listen to the provided ukulele version of the song, and use the TNT software to hear how it sounds to slide into and between chords. Try to emulate that on your uke. You can eliminate any unwanted noise made by the slide by muting with your other fingers; simply place those fingers on the strings behind the slide as you play.

Of course, if you don't have a slide, the song will sound fine without it. You can still emulate the sound of a slide by using your ring finger to barre and slide into chords that would have been played with a real slide.

☆ **FUN FACT** ☆

George Thorogood briefly played minor-league baseball for the Delaware Destroyers before he hit the big time playing the blues with another group of Destroyers—his band.

Bad to the Bone

Open G tuning:
④ = G ② = B
③ = D ① = G

Words and Music by
GEORGE THOROGOOD

Moderately ♩ = 98

Intro:

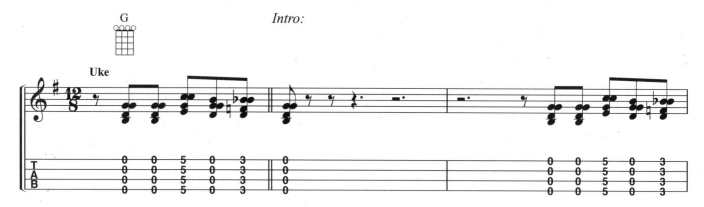

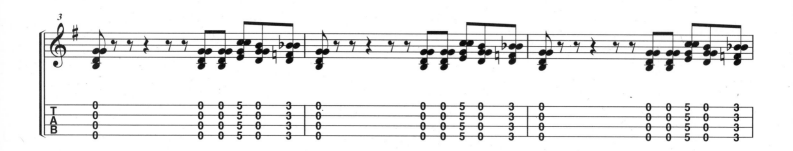

Band enters

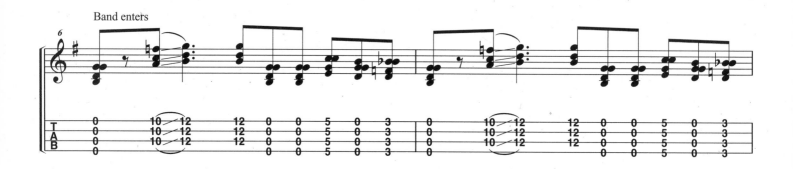

Coda

Outro:

Cont. rhy. simile

whoo,   bad   to the bone.

Play 4 times

trem. pick

Verse 2:
I broke a thousand hearts
Before I met you.
I'll break a thousand more, baby,
Before I am through.
I wanna be yours, pretty baby,
Yours and yours alone.
I'm here to tell ya, honey,
That I'm bad to the bone,
Bad to the bone.
B-b-b-b-b-b-b bad,
B-b-b-b-b-b-b bad.
B-b-b-b-b-b-b bad,
Bad to the bone.
(To Guitar Solo 1:)

Verse 4:
Now, when I walk the streets,
Kings and Queens step aside.
Every woman I meet, heh, heh,
They all stay satisfied.
I wanna tell you, pretty baby,
What I see I make my own.
And I'm here to tell ya, honey,
That I'm bad to the bone,
Bad to the bone.
B-b-b-b-b-b-b bad,
B-b-b-b-b-b-b bad.
B-b-b-b-b-b-b bad,
Whoo, bad to the bone.
(To Outro:)

Big Yellow Taxi

Joni Mitchell released "Big Yellow Taxi" on her 1970 album, *Ladies of the Canyon*. An upbeat strummer, the track contrasts with the slower and sometimes moodier tunes she was writing at the time. Mitchell was inspired to write the song during a stay in Hawaii. After arriving at a hotel one night, she opened the shades to find a huge parking lot in front of the hotel, obstructing the paradise she saw in the hills beyond. The studio recording of "Big Yellow Taxi" reached No. 67 on the Billboard Hot 100 in August 1970, and a live version released in 1975 climbed up to No. 32 on the same chart. The song has been covered many times, including versions by Bob Dylan and the Counting Crows.

The driving, percussive strumming patterns in "Big Yellow Taxi" give the song its upbeat feel. This percussive feel comes partly from the *scratch rhythms*—shown as "x" noteheads in the notation and TAB. To play scratch rhythm, lightly lift your fret-hand fingers off the strings just enough to dampen them, then strum. You should hear a percussive "chukka, chukka" sound. If you hear any actual notes, then you're still pushing down too much with your fret-hand fingers. This works best for chord shapes that require you to fret every note, because your fingers naturally dampen the string as you release the pressure. Scratch rhythms *can* be played from chords with open strings—like the A chord. Just be sure your fret-hand fingers are dampening all the strings. Use as little motion as possible; you want to be able to quickly pop your fingers back on the fretboard to grab the next chord. For your strumming hand, use your index finger to strike the strings. Using a pick may be too much on an exciting, upbeat tune like this.

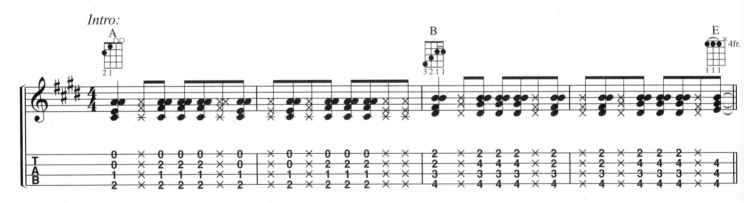

Intro:

TIP

Don't worry too much about when to play scratch rhythm, when to play chords, and when you need to leave strums out. If you do that, you may lose control of your strumming hand—and the groove of the song, which is the most important part! Move your strumming hand constantly in a down-and-up motion as you play. You can leave strums out by strumming through the air, which will make it easier for your strumming hand to stay in rhythm. If you listen to the original recording or the ukulele version to hear when there's scratch rhythm and when strums are left out, you'll master the groove before long! Remember, with the TNT software on the included CDs, you can loop a section of the recording and just play along until you feel comfortable with the rhythm.

"Big Yellow Taxi" has three basic chords: E, A, and B, with an occasional embellishment on the E chord. But the E, A, and B are the most important chords in the song; if you have trouble with the quick changes between E and A/E, you can always eliminate the A/E chords until you're comfortable playing them. The song will still sound fine.

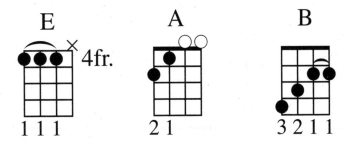

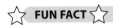

☆ **FUN FACT** ☆

The first "Earth Day" was in 1970, the same year this song was published. At the dawn of the environmental movement, Joni Mitchell came up with this simple, light-hearted tune with a whimsical warning: "They paved paradise, put up a parking lot."

Big Yellow Taxi

Words and Music by
JONI MITCHELL

paved par-a-dise, put up a park-ing lot.___

2. They   I said,

don't it al-ways seem___ to go   that you don't know what___ you've got___ till it's gone. They

paved par-a-dise, put up a park-ing lot.___   They

paved par-a-dise, put up a park-ing lot.___   They

paved par-a-dise,_ put up a park-ing lot.___

Verse 2:
They took all the trees,
Put 'em in a tree museum.
And they charged the people
A dollar and a half just to see 'em.
(To Chorus:)

Verse 3:
Hey farmer, farmer,
Put away that DDT now.
Give me spots on my apples,
But leave me the birds and the bees,
Please!
(To Chorus:)

Verse 4:
Late last night
I heard the screen door slam.
And a big yellow taxi
Took away my old man.
(To Chorus:)

Creep

Key Thoughts

"Creep" may have been been the song that put Radiohead on the international map, but it wasn't an overnight success. Included on the band's 1993 debut record, *Pablo Honey*, "Creep" was released as a single the year before but didn't start climbing the charts until several months after the album hit the shelves. Its success pushed *Pablo Honey* to No. 32 on the Billboard 200 album chart.

Take Note

Throughout the intro and verses, guitarist Ed O'Brien helps create a psychedelic backdrop with *arpeggios* of the chord shapes. These arpeggios have been adapted to ukulele, and you can pick the notes in two main ways, each employing the fingers. The example on the next page shows both options, using italic letters that tell you which finger to use for which note: *p* = thumb, *i* = index, *m* = middle, and *a* = ring.

The first way to play the arpeggios is to assign one finger to each string, with your thumb, index, middle, and ring fingers sticking to the 4th, 3rd, 2nd, and 1st strings, respectively. You can also play using just your thumb, index, and middle fingers to cover three consecutive strings as a unit. Since there are just four strings on a ukulele, that means your fingers will only have to move between two positions: the bottom three strings and the top three strings. For instance, in measure 1, start by playing the first three notes with your thumb, index, and middle fingers. Then, shift your fingers up a string set to grab the fourth note with your thumb, which leaves your hand in position to grab notes on the top three strings all the way through measure 2. Try out both techniques, but use whatever feels most comfortable to you.

DEFINITION

Any time you play the notes of a chord individually, you're playing an **arpeggio**. You can play the individual notes in any order to arpeggiate a chord, but they must be single notes; once you play two or more notes at the same time, you're no longer playing an arpeggio.

Also, note how O'Brien embellishes the B and C chords in the intro (highlighted in the following example). This briefly creates a sus chord, but it moves by so quickly that it's not notated in the chord frames and could easily be overlooked.

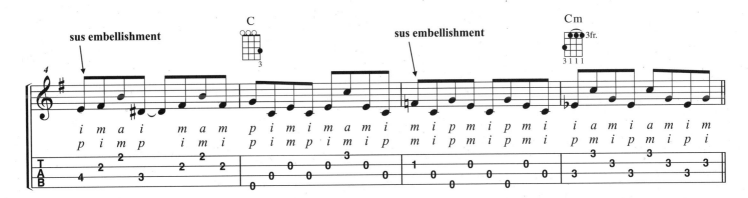

At the chorus, the accompaniment switches from arpeggiated chords to full strumming for extra punch. On top of this rhythm part, guitarist Jonny Greenwood brings the chorus to a climax by tremolo picking a rising pattern, which is adapted here to ukulele. To play it, emulate a pick with your index finger by supporting it with your thumb and projecting the fingertip downward. Then, simply move your hand up and down as quickly as you can without any discomfort. (For more on tremolo picking, see the performance notes to "Maggie May.")

☆ **FUN FACT** ☆

All the members of Radiohead were teenagers when they met at an all-boys school in 1985. Because they met on Fridays to play music, they called themselves "On a Friday," and they got their start in an Oxford pub called Jericho Tavern—the same place where their future managers, Chris Hufford and Bryce Edge, noticed them.

Creep

Words and Music by
THOMAS YORKE, JONATHAN GREENWOOD,
PHILIP SELWAY, COLIN GREENWOOD,
EDWARD O'BRIEN, ALBERT HAMMOND
and MIKE HAZELWOOD

I don't be - long_____ here.

Uke 1

trem. pick

Uke 3

2. I don't care if it hurts._____ here.

Oh,_____ oh._____

Cont. in slashes

You're so ver - y spe - cial.

I wish I was spe - cial... But I'm a_____ creep._

Chorus:

I'm a_____ weir - do._____

Uke 2

mp

What the hell am I do - ing here?____

I don't be - long_____ here, I don't be - long_____ here.

If You Could Read My Mind

Key Thoughts

Ontario-born Gordon Lightfoot performed on the folk circuit for over 10 years before becoming an "overnight" success in 1971 with the gentle ballad "If You Could Read My Mind."

Take Note

The accompaniment for "If You Could Read My Mind" is a fairly simple fingerpicking pattern that repeats throughout the song. For this pattern, assign your thumb to the 3rd string, your index finger to the 2nd string, and your middle finger to the 1st string. In the excerpt below, these fingerings are shown between notation and TAB to help you get your bearings. As is common throughout the fingerpicking world, Spanish abbreviations represent each finger: *p* (pulgar) = thumb; *i* (indice) = index; *m* (medio) = middle, and *a* (annular) = ring. In the intro, the last note of each measure is accented slightly, making those final notes ring into the next measure like a brief melody (the accented notes are shown below). Once you reach the verse, leave out the accents and the part will blend into the background more easily behind the vocals. Make sure to listen carefully to the included recording if you have trouble digesting any of this information. Remember, you can slow down and loop any section you want using the TNT software included on the CDs.

Intro:

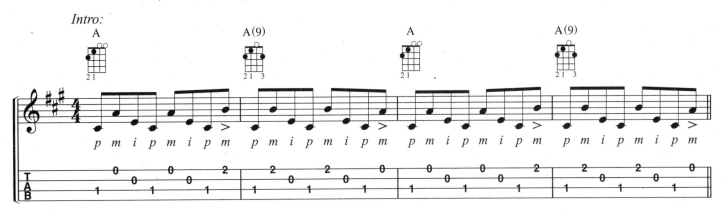

⭐ **FUN FACT** ⭐

Gordon Lightfoot's 1970 single "If You Could Read My Mind," from the poor-selling album *Sit Down Young Stranger*, became such a big hit that his record company decided to capitalize on the success and in 1971 renamed the album *If You Could Read My Mind*.

UKULELE STARS

While **KING DAVID KALAKAUA** of Hawaii lived several generations before Gordon Lightfoot, if you could read Kalakaua's mind, you'd likely see a picture of a Hawaiian nation with a strong cultural identity. Kalakaua played an integral part in lifting up Hawaiian tradition, despite the growing influence of external modern societies. The ukulele was introduced to the Hawaiians in 1879 under King Kalakaua's reign, and his highness used it to accompany the hula and during royal gatherings. Without his promotion of the instrument, it would not be as popular as it is today.

If You Could Read My Mind

Words and Music by
GORDON LIGHTFOOT

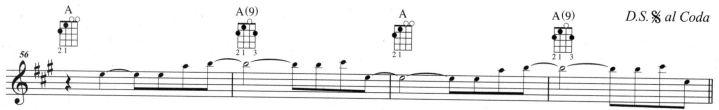

𝄌 *Coda*

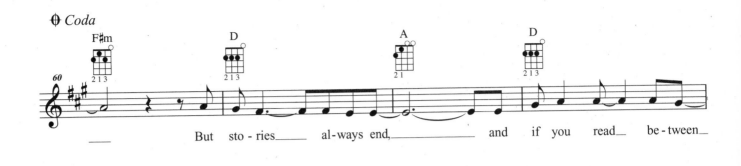

But sto - ries____ al - ways end,_____ and if you read__ be - tween__

____ the lines,_ you'll know that I'm__ just try - in' to un - der - stand____ the

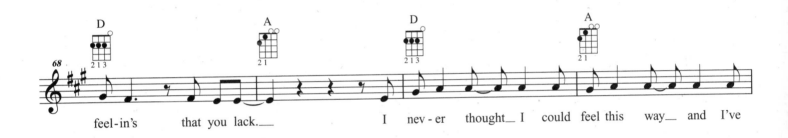

feel-in's____ that you lack.__ I nev - er thought__ I could feel this way__ and I've

got to say__ that I just don't get it. I don't know_ where we____ went wrong,_ but the

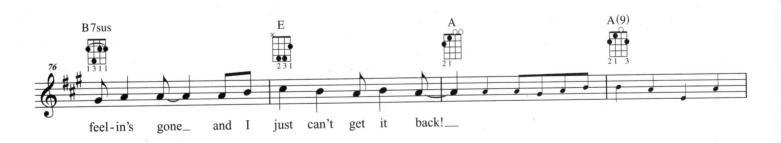

feel-in's gone__ and I just can't get it back!__

rit.

Do You Want to Know a Secret

Key Thoughts

"Do You Want to Know a Secret" first appeared on The Beatles' debut album, *Please Please Me*—a spirited record with a live feel tracked during only a few days at EMI's studios. The two previously released singles ("Please Please Me" and "Love Me Do") and their B-sides ("P.S. I Love You" and "Ask Me Why") were recorded on separate occasions, but all 10 of the other tracks were recorded in one marathon session in February 1963. "Do You Want to Know a Secret" was subsequently released as a single in 1964, and climbed to No. 2 on the Billboard Hot 100 chart.

Take Note

"Do You Want to Know a Secret" starts with a slow intro backed by held chords. Notice the tremolo strums in the original recording for the Em and G chords in measures 3 and 4; unlike the single-note tremolo picking found in "Maggie May," these are full-chord strums. Also, instead of a pick, use your index finger to brush quickly up and down the strings. Hold your hand steady, point your index finger back toward the bridge, and strum with your finger straight but bent at the knuckle.

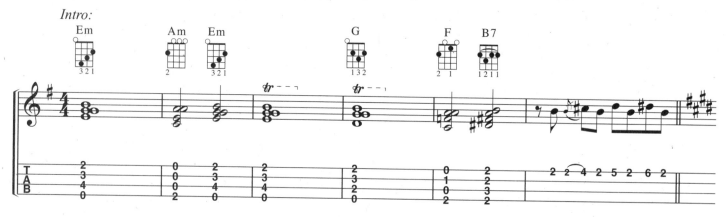

For the verse pattern, in general, you should assign your thumb, index, and middle fingers to the 3rd, 2nd, and 1st strings, respectively. For the E chord, pluck the first two notes with your thumb and index finger, then play both strums on the second beat with your index finger brushing down then up across the strings. For the G♯m and Gm chords, pluck the bass note on the 3rd string with your thumb, then pluck the following *double stop* on the first two strings with your index and middle fingers. Plucking these two chords gives a bouncier sound than if you tried to strum between each bass note. Then, for the following F♯m and B chords, play them the same way you did the G♯m and Gm chords—with finger strums on the last two eighth notes of each chord. (For a complete discussion of right-hand fingerings, see the lesson for "If You Could Read My Mind.")

DEFINITION

A **double stop** is any two fretted notes played together (double = two strings; stop = stopping a string). The term likely came from the classical music world via the fretless stringed instruments—like violin and viola—where your fingers, not the frets, actually "stop" the strings by pressing them into the fretboard.

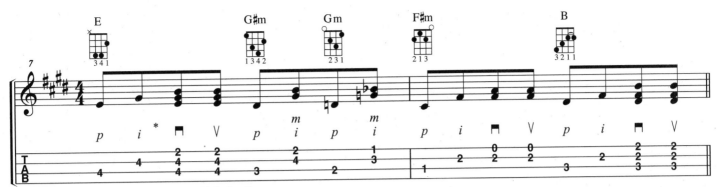

*Strum with index finger.

⭐ **FUN FACT** ⭐

At 10 p.m., after a full day of recording songs for *Please Please Me*, The Beatles still needed to record one more tune, but they didn't know what it should be. They took a break and decided to record "Twist and Shout," with John Lennon singing lead. Since Lennon had a cold and nearly no voice left after singing all day, the band didn't have too much of an opportunity left to record the song. But they nailed it on the first take, and that recording—with Lennon's shredded vocals—became the definitive version of the song.

Do You Want to Know a Secret

Slowly

Intro:

Words and Music by
JOHN LENNON and PAUL McCARTNEY

© 1963 (Renewed) NORTHERN SONGS LTD. (UK)
All Rights in the U.S. and Canada Controlled by EMI UNART CATALOG INC. (Publishing) and ALFRED PUBLISHING CO., INC. (Print)
All Rights Reserved

Don't Stop Believin'

Key Thoughts

Journey broke through to the mainstream in 1981 with the multi-platinum album *Escape*. Powered by *three* top-10 singles, *Escape* climbed to No. 1 on the Billboard 200. The leadoff track—and second single—is "Don't Stop Believin'," a dramatic rocker that opens over a ballad-like piano backdrop before kicking into arena-rock mode when the drums enter at the chorus.

Take Note

A keyboard figure drives the verses of "Don't Stop Believin'," and this part has been adapted to ukulele in the arrangement. To get the feel of a pianist rocking between chords and single notes, pluck the strings with your fingers instead of using a pick. Assign your thumb, index, and middle fingers to the 3rd, 2nd, and 1st strings, respectively. In the following example, *p* = thumb, *i* = index, and *m* = middle. Note how the pattern is always the same from chord to chord, with your index finger doing double duty on the 2nd string.

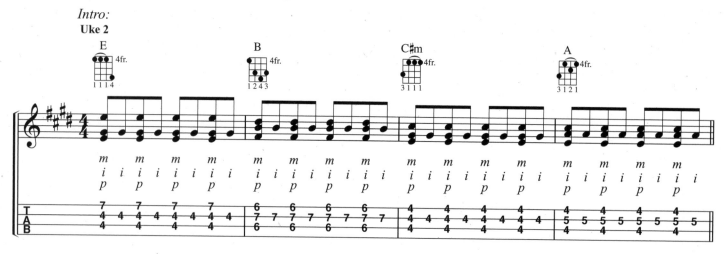

Starting at the interlude at measure 25, guitarist Neal Schon gradually builds into a scorching guitar lick. While not included in the following arrangement of the song, this lick has been adapted to ukulele on the provided recording and is also shown below. If you want to learn it, don't get too caught up with the note values. The first measure repeats multiple times, gradually speeding up until the very last measure of the interlude, when you jump up to grab the note in the second measure below. Don't forget to use the TNT software on the included CDs to isolate and repeat this section until you get a feel for how it's supposed to sound. If you're more comfortable with a pick, try playing with a constant down-up pattern, as shown below. And if you opt to pluck with your fingers instead, try alternating between two fingers on the same string, like the middle and index fingers as shown below. This way, you'll be able to pick much more quickly than you would by using just one finger. For your fretting hand, use one finger per note, all along the same string. Play the lick as slowly as necessary to fret and play each note cleanly, then gradually speed it up.

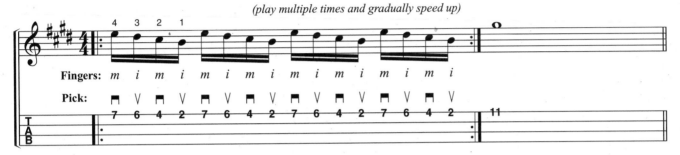

(play multiple times and gradually speed up)

☆ **FUN FACT** ☆

Journey guitarist Neal Schon was only 19 when Journey formed, but he was already an accomplished guitarist. In 1971—at the age of 17—Schon had joined Santana, playing guitar on three classic Santana records. Reportedly, he was recruited by Eric Clapton, as well, to be a member of Derek & the Dominos, but had already accepted Santana's offer. Schon left Santana to form Journey with another member of Santana's band: keyboardist Gregg Rolie.

Don't Stop Believin'

Words and Music by
JONATHAN CAIN, NEAL SCHON
and STEVE PERRY

Gimme Some Lovin'

The height of The Spencer Davis Group's popularity was sandwiched into a small window in the late '60s, during the years that Steve Winwood was in the band. Bolstered by Winwood's searing vocals, "Gimme Some Lovin' " was the band's biggest hit, and it climbed up to No. 7 on the Billboard Hot 100 chart.

The opening lick features a single-note line that rocks between G notes an *octave* apart. Play the high G on the 10th fret of the 1st string using your pinky finger, then reach down with your index finger to grab the low G on the 7th fret of the 3rd string. To beef up the lick, make sure to pair that low G with the open 4th string.

DEFINITION

An **octave** is the distance between two notes of the same pitch occurring in different registers. There are 12 half steps between notes an octave apart; each half step is the distance of a fret on your ukulele, making an octave a 12-fret distance.

Since the ukulele has little sustain, a riff like this can easily get lost in the mix. One way to add even more punch to the notes is to dampen a nearby string and play through it. You won't hear the note, but you *will* hear the extra attack from playing that other string—adding a little thump to the sound. On the provided recording, that extra punch has been added to the low G notes by dampening the 2nd string. You can do this by rolling your index finger downward, so that it's muting the 2nd string while also fretting the 3rd string. Then pluck through all three bottom strings.

Intro:

The song's signature organ lick has been adapted to ukulele in the arrangement. Organs have unlimited sustain, and this lick poses a problem because it features notes held out for more than a measure. But the B-3 organ used on the original recording employs a rotating Leslie speaker, so play each note multiple times; that will emulate the sound of the rotating speaker while also giving us the sustain we need.

☆ FUN FACT ☆

Singer Steve Winwood sounds like an old, experienced R&B singer on "Gimme Some Lovin', " but he was actually just a teenager when the song was recorded.

Gimme Some Lovin'

Words and Music by
STEVE WINWOOD, MUFF WINWOOD
and SPENCER DAVIS

Moderately fast ♩ = 147

Intro:

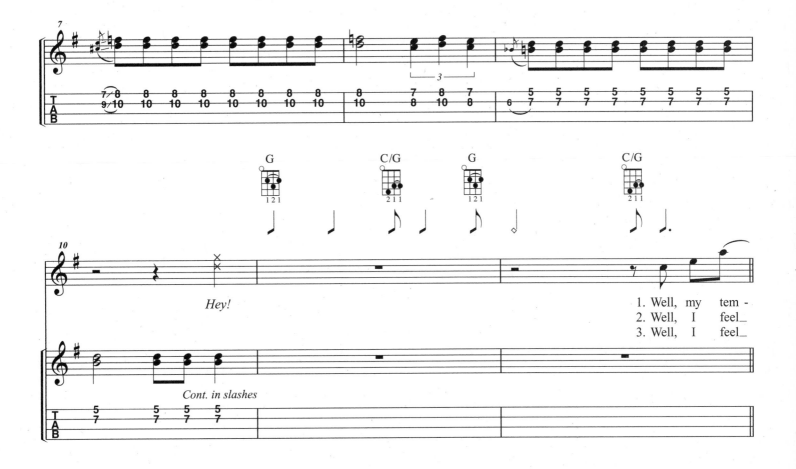

Hey!

1. Well, my tem-
2. Well, I feel
3. Well, I feel

Cont. in slashes

*w/Lead vocal ad lib. on repeats.

Good Riddance
(Time of Your Life)

American punk band Green Day struck a mellow, reflective pose with "Good Riddance (Time of Your Life)." Released in the period between the band's 1994 breakout success and their 2004 rise to mega-superstar status with *American Idiot*, this introspective acoustic ballad (with strings!) was a 180-degree about-face for the band heretofore known for edgy hard-driving rock.

Billie Joe Armstrong plays the guitar on "Good Riddance" in a casual, arpeggiated fashion, and you can reproduce this feeling on the uke. Strum down with your index finger over the neck of the ukulele, emphasizing the bass strings, then repeat the down-strum and quickly follow it with an up-strum across all the strings. Next, individually pick strings 2–3–2 with your index finger using an up-stroke, down-stroke, and up-stroke (respectively)—*or* use your middle finger to pluck the 2nd string and your index to pluck the 3rd. Now you've got the basic arpeggio pattern of the introduction, first verse, and chorus. Try it slowly at first, then gradually build up speed until you can play along with the provided recording without a second thought. Notice that the notation omits doubled notes for ease of reading, but the tablature includes these notes (that's why some chords have only two notes in the notation and three notes in the TAB).

Intro:

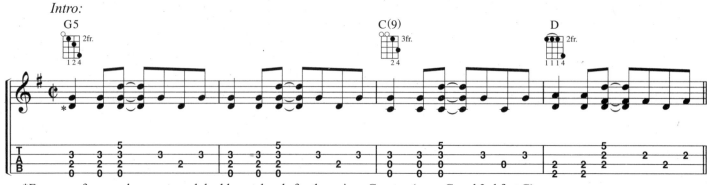

*For ease of use we have not used double noteheads for the unison G notes (open G and 3rd fret G). Refer to the TAB for the correct fingerings.

DEFINITION

"Good Riddance (Time of Your Life)" is played in **cut time**. Indicated by this ¢ symbol, cut time doubles up the tempo by counting only *two* beats per measure, not four. This means that you're counting one beat for each half note, as notated in the tempo marking at the top of the page: ♩ = 86 (86 beats per minute, half note gets the beat).

From measure 13 all the way through to the outro, you have the option of strumming the chords, arpeggiating each chord throughout, or breaking the monotony and giving the performance more dynamic interest by picking one part and strumming rhythm on another. When strumming, use the pattern below. Notice that instead of the G5 and C(9) chords employed in the arpeggiated introduction, full chords should be used throughout when strumming. However, like in the arpeggiated intro, you should still emphasize the bass strings of each chord with a down-stroke on the first beat of each measure.

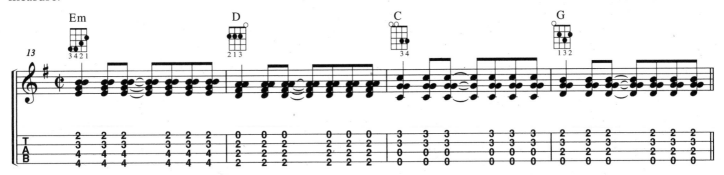

To finish, play the intro arpeggios for a return to a softer style at the outro.

 TIP

In the beginning of the song, see how the 4th finger remains stationary on the 5th fret of the 1st string for the G5, C(9), and D chords? Don't move that finger. Keep it planted firmly in place, and always try to minimize the movement of your fingers at all times. The same holds true for the 2nd finger on the 2nd fret of the 2nd string for the G5 and C(9) chords. As a general rule, when two sequential chords share a note, try not to remove that finger from the fretboard as you transition from one chord to the next; that way, you'll be able to make smoother and quicker chord changes.

☆ **FUN FACT** ☆

"Good Riddance (Time of Your Life)" was featured over a retrospective montage on the final episode of *Seinfeld* in 1998.

Good Riddance
(Time of Your Life)

Lyrics by
BILLIE JOE

Music by
BILLIE JOE and GREEN DAY

Bright in 2 ♩ = 86

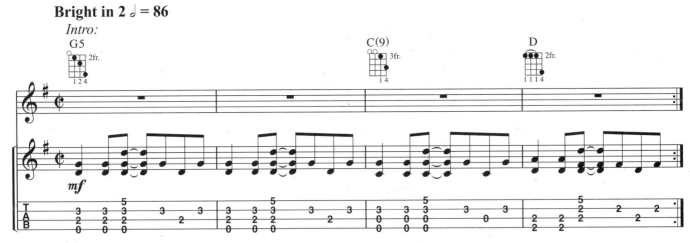

*For ease of use we have not used double noteheads for the unison G notes (open G and 3rd fret G).
Refer to the TAB for the correct fingerings.

1. An-oth-er turn-ing point, a fork stuck in the road.
2. So take the pho-to-graphs and still frames stuck in your mind.
3. *Instrumental*

Time grabs you by the wrist, di-rects
Hang it on a shelf in good

Interlude:

1.2.

3.

It's

Hotel California

Key
Thoughts

Eagles reportedly spent eight months in the studio working on their fifth release, *Hotel California*. The hard work paid off, and the album became an all-time top-20 seller in the U.S. This was the band's first outing with guitarist Joe Walsh, who replaced Bernie Leadon and injected more of a rock sound into their songs via his harder-edged electric guitar riffs and solos.

Take
Note

The intro figure takes work to master. This part was played on a 12-string acoustic guitar on the original recording, and the arrangement for ukulele is laid out in a way that, at first glance, might not seem intuitive. Listen carefully to the provided recording, then play along—and slow it down with the TNT software if you need to.

As an easier alternative, you can create a similar effect by holding the chord shapes and picking out a recurring pattern. The following example shows one way to do this. Pluck the four-note chord with all four fingers, then move your hand up so your thumb, index, and middle fingers cover the 3rd, 2nd, and 1st strings for the remainder of each measure. For an explanation of the italic letters in between the notation and TAB in this option, see the lesson for "If You Could Read My Mind."

Intro:

At the chorus, the rhythm moves into a strummed reggae beat. Strum through the muted strings for any "x" notes (all of which occur on the beat), then strum the chords on the final two sixteenth notes of each beat. Listen to the recording to get a feel for how this sounds, and remember that you can loop sections with the TNT software to play them over and over until you get the hang of it.

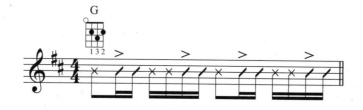

The dueling guitar lead line at the end of the song is included in this ukulele arrangement, and these phrases use *pull-offs* just like in the original recording. If you have trouble with the pull-offs, you can make the phrases easier by playing them across three-string shapes, as shown below. Use your thumb, index, and middle fingers to play these shapes.

DEFINITION

A **pull-off** is a note articulated with your fretting hand. To play a pull-off, start by fretting two notes simultaneously on the same string, then pluck the string as usual to sound the first note. Next, pull the finger fretting the higher note downward so that it plucks the string, but keep the other fretting finger in place; this action will sound the lower note.

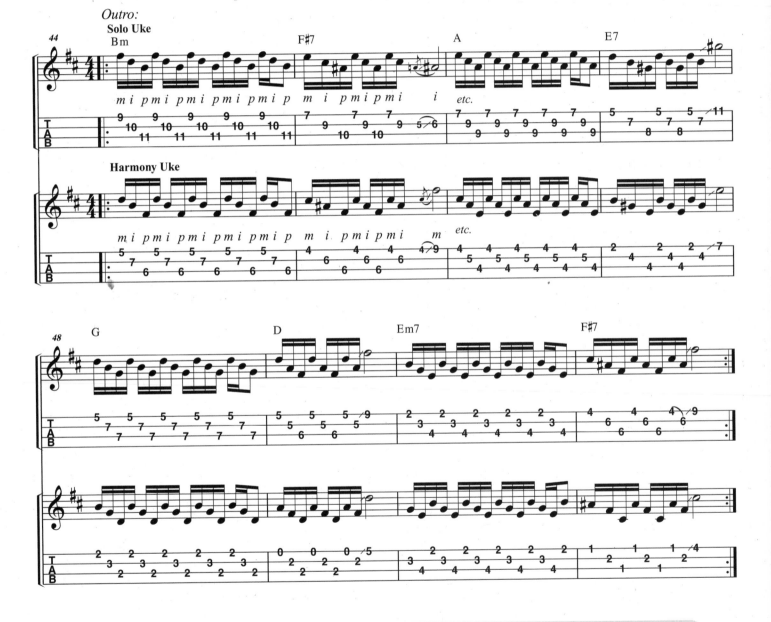

FUN FACT

On the original vinyl release of *Hotel California*, the words "V.O.L.: is five piece live" are inscribed on side 2, on the inside of the run-out groove. This somewhat cryptic quote means that the song "Victim of Love" was recorded live in one take as a five-piece band.

Hotel California

Words and Music by
DON HENLEY, GLENN FREY
and DON FELDER

Moderately slow ♩ = 74

Intro:

Bm   F#7   A   E7

G   D   Em7   F#7

Verse:

Bm

Uke cont. simile
Play slash rhythm on D.S.

F#7

1. On a dark des-ert high - way,__ cool__ wind in my hair,
2. Her mind is Tif - fan-y twist - ed.__ She got the Mer - ce-des bends.
3. *See additional lyrics*

A   E7

Cont. rhy. simile

warm__ smell__ of co - li - tas__ ris - ing up through the air._____
She got a lot of pret-ty, pret-ty boys that she calls friends.

G   D

Up a-head in the dis - tance I saw a shim - mer - ing light.
How they dance in the court - yard, sweet sum - mer sweat.

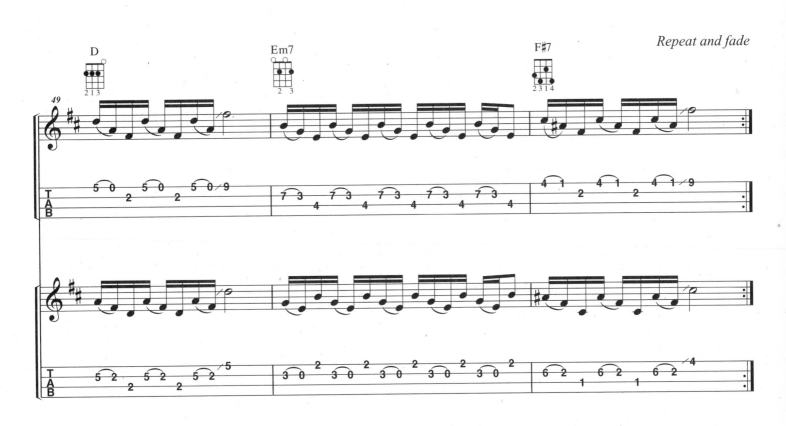

Repeat and fade

Verse 3:
Mirrors on the ceiling, the pink champagne on ice.
And she said, "We are all just prisoners here of our own device."
And in the master's chambers they gathered for the feast.
They stab it with their steely knives but they just can't kill the beast.
Last thing I remember I was running for the door.
I had to find the passage back to the place I was before.
"Relax," said the nightman, "We are programmed to receive."
You can check out anytime you like but you can never leave.

I'll See You in My Dreams

"I'll See You in My Dreams" is a classic song written by Isham Jones and Gus Kahn in 1924. Jones recorded the song with The Ray Miller Orchestra, and it was a chart success in 1925. Over the years, the song has been covered by a host of musicians, including Louis Armstrong, Ella Fitzgerald, Chet Atkins, and Django Reinhardt. The version of the song featured here closely follows Joe Brown's rendition, which he played on ukulele at the *Concert for George* in 2002—a tribute to The Beatles' George Harrison.

On the ukulele, most songs are strummed with the fingers of your right hand. But you might find that using a pick for "I'll See You in My Dreams" helps highlight the inner lines—like the rising notes on the 3rd string during the F chords in the opening measures. The included recording of this song features pick strumming to help highlight these inner lines. If you look at the notation and tablature, you'll notice that sometimes only three notes are shown in the notation, while four notes are shown in the TAB. This is because some notes are *unisons*, and omitting them from the notation makes it easier to read.

DEFINITION

Whenever you play two of the same notes together, you're playing a **unison**. When multiple instruments play the same melodic lines and notes together, they're also playing in unison.

Intro:

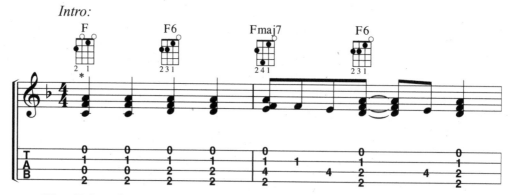

*Note: To keep the music notation easy to read, unison notes (same note/same octave) are indicated only once in the notation but are shown clearly in the TAB and chord grids.

To emulate the sound on the provided recording, you'll need to add a bouncy swing feel to your strums. You can do this by quickly dampening the strings after you strike a chord. For chords with no open strings, dampen the strings by slightly lifting your left hand fingers off the fretboard.

You can dampen chords with open strings several ways: by rolling your fretting fingers up or down enough to mute the strings, by using the free fingers on your fretting hand to lightly dampen all the strings, or by using the heel of your picking hand. Play the song with a loose feel, and notice that single-note lines and tied chords are held, not dampened. For instance, in the following line, try adding the bounce to the first three measures, then let the 4th measure ring out. Again, listen to the provided recording to get a sense of how it should sound.

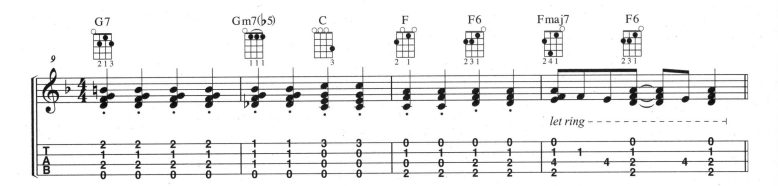

Practice these string-dampening techniques and compare your sound to the recorded version until you can produce the same bounce.

UKULELE STARS

Beatle **GEORGE HARRISON** was an avid ukulele player, and his interest in the instrument —along with his fame—helped inspire the current generation of ukulele players. Harrison, himself, was inspired by comedian/musician George Formby, who played the banjolele (an instrument that's built like a uke, but sounds like a banjo). Clips of Harrison playing ukulele can be found on YouTube, including one of Harrison singing "Ain't She Sweet" with Paul McCartney and Ringo Starr. Before they hit the big time, The Beatles recorded "Ain't She Sweet" in Hamburg with John Lennon singing lead.

I'll See You in My Dreams

Words by GUS KAHN
Music by ISHAM JONES

Medium swing

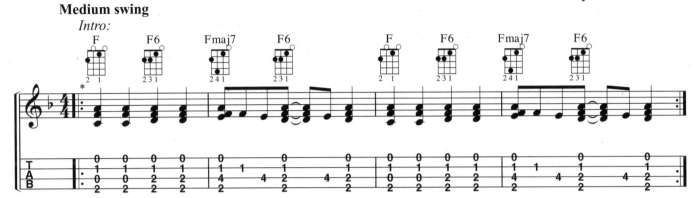

*Note: To keep the music notation easy to read, unison notes (same note/same octave)
are indicated only once in the notation but are shown clearly in the TAB and chord grids.

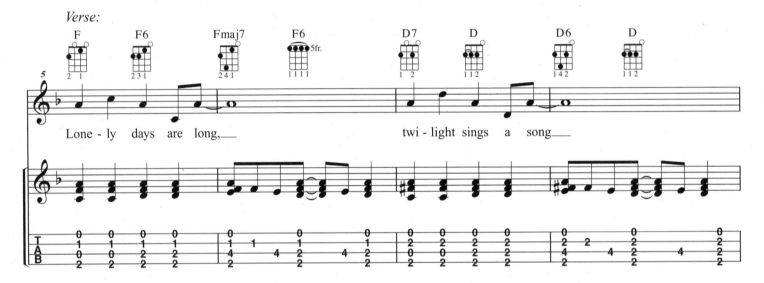

Lone - ly days are long,___ twi - light sings a song___

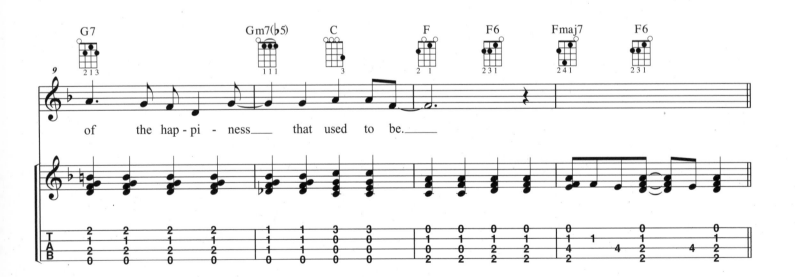

of the hap - pi - ness___ that used to be.___

Layla
(*Unplugged* version)

Key Thoughts

In 1992, Eric Clapton appeared to completely reinvent his signature song, "Layla," for his *MTV Unplugged* special. Performed on acoustic guitars with a lazy shuffle feel minus the original driving signature riff, this version was so different from the original that Clapton told the audience, "See if you can spot this one." The truth is, Clapton originally conceived the song in 1970 as a slow blues shuffle, exactly as performed at the show. But after he had presented it to Duane Allman and his bandmates for a Derek & the Dominos recording session, Duane suggested they turn it into an up-tempo rocker, adding the now-famous opening riff used in the electric version.

Take Note

The song has an underlying *shuffle* feel, meaning that the eighth notes are played with the first note long and the second note short, instead of exactly even. This long-short rhythm is based around a triplet pulse. Writing out all the triplets can make the music look more complicated than it is, so the triplet feel icon is often shown at the top of the piece, and eighth notes are written without the triplet indication. In this case, every time you see two eighth notes, play them as if the first one has the length of the first two notes of a triplet, and the last eighth note gets the value of the last note in a triplet. This is notated in musical terms below. But don't get too lost in these technical concepts. It's important to *feel* it, so listen carefully to the provided recording and imitate it.

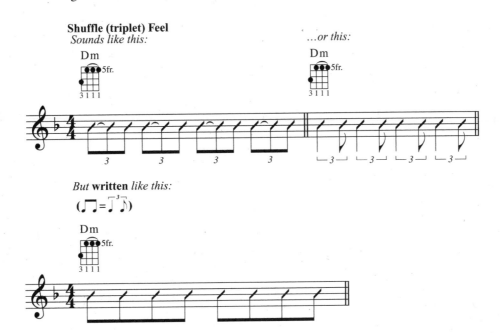

The main accompaniment is a two-bar pattern, shown below with an initial pick-up. It's right up front in the intro, repeated in each chorus, and can be played throughout the guitar solo section. Follow the left hand fingerings as indicated in the notation and chord frames.

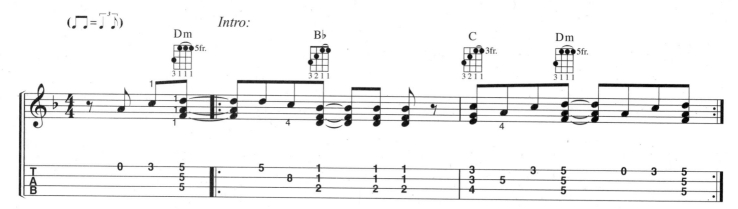

☆ **FUN FACT** ☆

"Layla" is based on an ancient Persian love poem called "Layla and Majnun," in which Majnun goes mad after Layla's father forbids her from marrying Majnun. Like Majnun, Clapton was going mad because he was in love with his good friend's wife. This friend happened to be George Harrison of The Beatles, and Harrison's wife was Pattie Boyd. Clapton wrote "Layla" at the height of his infatuation, and Clapton and Boyd later married, but divorced after 10 years. In the end, Boyd became the subject of *three* of rock's greatest songs: Clapton's "Layla," "Wonderful Tonight," and Harrison's "Something."

Layla
(*Unplugged* version)

Words and Music by
ERIC CLAPTON and JIM GORDON

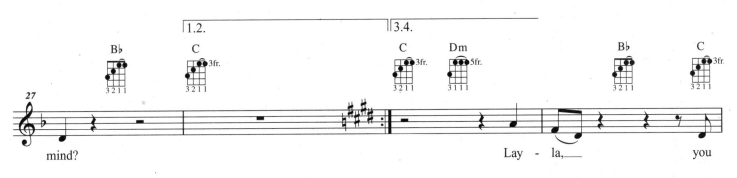

mind?   Lay - la,___   you

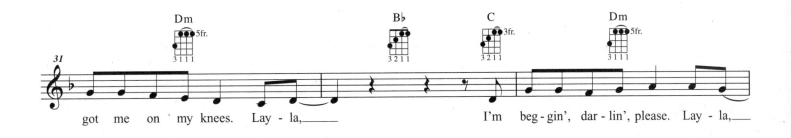

got me on my knees. Lay - la,___   I'm beg - gin', dar - lin', please. Lay - la,___

To Coda ⊕

___   dar - ling, won't you ease my wor - ried   mind?

Guitar Solo:

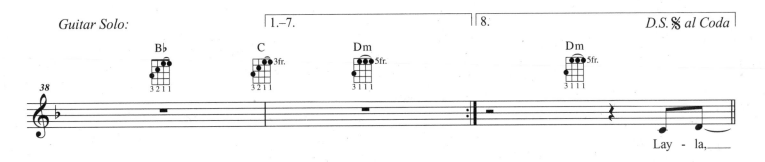

Lay - la,___

⊕ *Coda*

Freely

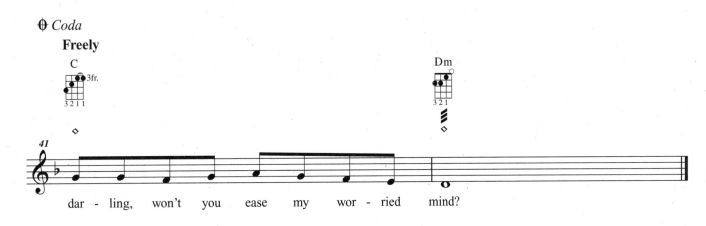

dar - ling, won't you ease my wor - ried   mind?

Long Train Runnin'

"Long Train Runnin'" was The Doobie Brothers' third-straight top-five single. Track two of their 1973 release *The Captain and Me*, this song features a funky groove built from a rhythmic, strummed guitar riff. Originally played up the neck on an electric guitar by the song's writer and singer, Tom Johnston, this distinctive riff translates well to ukulele with easier fingerings down at the nut.

By including *scratch rhythm* (the sound made when strings muted by fret-hand fingers are strummed), the driving strums in "Long Train Runnin'" keep the momentum going even when chords are not strummed. (For a more detailed discussion of scratch rhythm, see the performance notes for "Big Yellow Taxi.")

Strum the chords with your index finger over the neck of the ukulele, since a pick can easily overpower the strings. Pay close attention to how the *hammer-ons* sound on the recording. You can also count along, as shown in the figure below. If you have trouble with the tricky rhythms, play along with the provided ukulele recording of the song. Remember—you can slow it down with the TNT software and gradually work up to normal speed, and also loop sections for practice. Don't get too worried about all the notes and "x"s. The most important thing is that you *hear* it, so spend some quality time with the recording.

DEFINITION

When you articulate a note by tapping down on a fret with your left hand, you're playing a **hammer-on**. You usually pluck another note on the same string just before executing the hammer-on; if you look at the first measure of "Long Train Runnin'," you'll see that the opening chord is strummed before the hammer-on. In this case, *two* hammer-ons are played simultaneously—on the 1st and 3rd strings.

In verses 3, 5, and 6, some of the downbeats are punctuated by sliding the Gm shape down to F♯m for a strum or two, highlighting the return to Gm at the beginning of the next bar. In the notation, these variations are shown at the bottom of the page, within two boxes labeled "Rhy. Fig. 1" and "Rhy. Fig. 2." They're also shown below for your convenience. Notice how both of these figures move down to that F♯m chord, but each has a distinctive rhythmic variation.

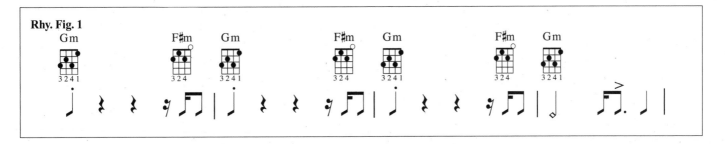

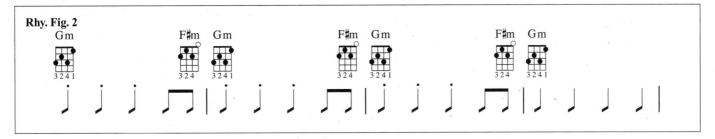

☆ **FUN FACT** ☆

"Long Train Runnin'" came out of a jam that The Doobie Brothers regularly performed long before the tune was crafted. They called this early version "Rosie Pig Moseley."

UKULELE STARS

The Doobie Brothers are a classic rock band, and just as there are plenty of classic rock bands from the '60s and '70s, there are plenty of classic ukulele players from even earlier time periods. One of these classic uke players is **ROY SMECK**, who played on over 500 recordings, mostly in the 1920s and 1930s. Smeck was a multi-instrumentalist so adept at ukulele, banjo, guitar, and steel guitar that he was often called the "Wizard of the Strings." A pure entertainer, Smeck spent time on the vaudeville circuit and played his instruments with theatrical flair.

Long Train Runnin'

Tempo ♩ = 116

Words and Music by
TOM JOHNSTON

1. Down a - round__ the cor - ner, half a mile__ from here,__ you

2.–6. *See additional lyrics*

see them old trains run - nin' and you watch them dis - ap - pear.__ With - out

A tempo

Verse 2:
You know I saw Miss Lucy,
Down along the tracks;
She lost her home and her family,
And she won't be comin' back.
Without love, where would you be right now,
Without love?

Verses 3 & 5:
Well, the Illinois Central
And the Southern Central freight,
Gotta keep on pushin', mama,
'Cause you know they're runnin' late.
Without love, where would you be right now,
Without love?
(1st time to Verse 4:)
(2nd time to Verse 6:)

Verse 4:
Instrumental Solo
(To Verse 5:)

Verse 6:
Where pistons keep on churnin'
And the wheels go 'round and 'round,
And the steel rails are cold and hard
For the miles that they go down.
Without love, where would you be right now,
Without love?
(To Coda)

Moondance

The title track from Van Morrison's February 1970 album, "Moondance" has become a staple of classic-rock radio. Curiously, the song wasn't an instant success, though a large part of this may be because it wasn't initially released as a single. It's a testament to the song's power that it still managed to find its way onto the Billboard Hot 100 chart—seven years later!

Van Morrison provides a rhythm foundation in the verses by strumming a repeated Am–Bm7–Am7–Bm7 chord progression. Follow the suggested fingerings, and your hand will be in perfect position for each chord. Start by holding down the only fretted note of the Am chord with your index finger, then barre your index finger across the same fret for Bm7. The following Am7 shape might feel more comfortable if you use the index, ring, and middle fingers on the 1st, 2nd, and 3rd strings, respectively. But by using the suggested fingering with your middle, pinky, and ring fingers on the 1st, 2nd, and 3rd strings, your hand will be in perfect position to simply slap down the index finger on the 2nd fret for the following Bm7 chord.

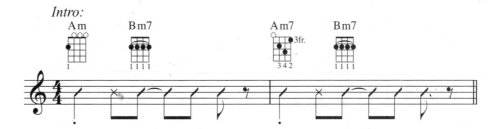

If you find this move a little difficult, you can instead alternate between the root-position Am chord and the Bm7 chord throughout, since the Am7 chord is really just an extended Am chord. This will sound fine until you can work the three-chord version up to speed.

At the chorus, Morrison plays some *syncopated* chord stabs on guitar (to *syncopate* means to accent the weak beats). For this ukulele arrangement, we'll execute this with a barred Dm chord and a four-fingered Am chord. Notice how Morrison does this by playing heavy strums on the eighth note before the strongest beats (beats 1 and 3) of each measure. If you find switching these shapes is difficult, you can always substitute root-position versions of these chords, like the ones below.

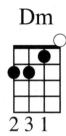

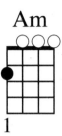

TIP

Pay close attention to the quarter-note triplets just before the chorus and in the final line of the song. Quarter-note triplets fit three equal notes into the space of two quarter notes, and this can be a difficult rhythm to feel. Play along with the included recording to get the hang of this. Use the TNT software to slow things down until you feel the rhythm internally, and then speed the song up to performance tempo.

FUN FACT

Cover versions of "Moondance" have been recorded by literally *hundreds* of acts. The universal appeal of this song lends itself to a diversity of styles, and you'll find recorded vocal and instrumental versions from a wide range of artists such as Greg Brown, Sun Ra, Michael Bublé, Nana Mouskouri, Bobby McFerrin, Andreas Vollenweider, Kathie Lee Gifford, and countless others.

UKULELE STARS

While Van Morrison is one of pop and rock music's most prominent heroes, **ERNEST KAAI** stands tall as one of the ukulele world's greatest heroes. Kaai helped spread the ukulele's popularity with worldwide virtuosic performances in the first few decades of the 1900s. He also operated a ukulele manufacturing company *and* published a ukulele method. A multitalented teacher, performer, and recording artist, Kaai was also proficient on guitar and mandolin.

Moondance

Words and Music by
VAN MORRISON

Maggie May

Prior to "Maggie May," raspy-voiced Rod Stewart had enjoyed some success as both the vocalist for the Jeff Beck Group and frontman for the band Faces. But it was this inadvertent chart-topper that really launched Rod's solo career in 1971. The song was originally released as the B-side to his "Reason to Believe" single. When British DJs began playing the flip side instead of the intended A-side, "Maggie May" began its ascendancy to rock classic status.

Co-written by Stewart and Martin Quittenton, the lyrics are a largely autobiographical tale of a young man's sexual relationship with an older woman.

"Maggie May" has the distinction of being one of the first rock songs to feature a mandolin, making it an unwitting precursor to Led Zeppelin's "The Battle of Evermore." The mandolin on the record was played by British folk-rock musician Ray Jackson.

The intro features strummed chords along with a few individual notes that highlight a short melody, one that can be hard to pick out by looking at the music. In measure 2, highlight the 3rd string, the same string where the pull-off happens from the 4th to the 2nd fret. In measure 3, highlight the top string in each chord—these notes make up that short melody. While picking out the individual notes of each chord, keep your fingers in the chord shape and allow the notes to ring throughout. If you have trouble following the notation, make sure to listen carefully to the provided recording, and use the TNT software to slow things down.

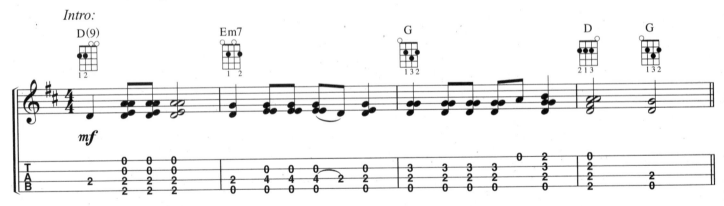

The verse and guitar solo sections are simple exercises in strumming open-position chords. On the provided recording, we've arranged the guitar solos for ukulele, though they're not shown in the notation and TAB. This is a good opportunity for you to use your ear to learn some parts. Use the TNT software to slow things down or loop sections if you need to. Have fun!

Try playing the mandolin part in the coda with a pick. This section makes use of *tremolo picking*. You might find it helpful to rotate from your wrist in a quick up-and-down manner, moving mostly your hand as opposed to your whole arm.

DEFINITION

Tremolo picking is a technique in which you quickly pick a single note over and over. The technique is sometimes shown over long notes with several diagonal lines cutting across the stem of a note (or above or below a whole note, which doesn't have stems). You often hear tremolo picking in classical guitar and surf music.

☆ **FUN FACT** ☆

Since "Maggie May" was a B-side (in the era of the three-minute pop song), it never received any form of an edit for airplay and became one of the few five-minute-plus songs to make it into regular rotation on Top 40 radio.

Maggie May

Words and Music by
ROD STEWART and
MARTIN QUITTENTON

Mag - gie, I could-n't have tried__ an - y - more._____   You

*D/F♯ 2nd and 3rd time only.

led me a - way from__ home   just to save you from be-ing a - lone.   You

stole my heart__ and that's__ what real - ly hurts.__   2. The

Solo 1:

D.S. 𝄋 al Coda

⊕ *Coda*   *Solo 2:*

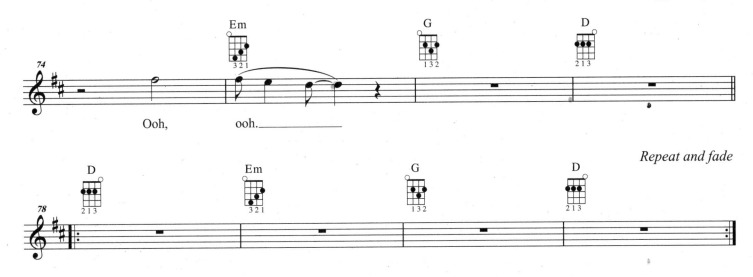

Ooh,   ooh._____

Repeat and fade

Verse 2:
The morning sun, when it's in your face,
Really shows your age.
But that don't worry me none,
In my eyes you're everything.
I laughed at all of your jokes,
My love you didn't need to coax.
Oh, Maggie, I couldn't have tried anymore.
You lead me away from home
Just to save you from being alone.
You stole my soul and that's a
Pain I can do without.

Verse 3:
All I needed was a friend
To lend a guiding hand.
But you turned into a lover and, mother,
What a lover, you wore me out.
All you did was wreck my bed,
And in the morning kick me in the head.
Oh, Maggie, I couldn't have tried anymore.
You lead me away from home
'Cause you didn't want to be alone.
You stole my heart,
I couldn't leave you if I tried.
(To Solo 1:)

Verse 4:
I suppose I could collect my books
And get on back to school.
Or steal my daddy's cue,
And make a living out of playing pool.
Or find myself a rock and roll band
That needs a helping hand.
Oh, Maggie, I wish I'd never seen your face.
You made a first-class fool out of me,
But I'm as blind as a fool can be.
You stole my heart
But I love you anyway.
(To Solo 2:)

Over the Rainbow

This song has become such a part of the American fabric that it almost needs no introduction. Penned by Harold Arlen and Yip Harburg in 1939 for *The Wizard of Oz*, "Over the Rainbow" became famous with Judy Garland's performance. Since that time, countless versions have been recorded in every imaginable genre. The song was voted No. 1 in the "Songs of the Century" poll done by the Recording Industry Association of America and the National Endowment for the Arts, and it was listed as the greatest movie song of all time by the American Film Institute. Lyrics from the song have even been featured on a U.S. postage stamp along with a picture of lyricist Yip Harburg.

The version of "Over the Rainbow" in this book is based on a recording by Hawaiian singer Israel "Iz" Kamakawiwoʻole. Arranged with only vocals and ukulele, Iz's rendition has been featured in many movies and television shows since being recorded in 1993, including *Finding Forrester*, *50 First Dates*, *Meet Joe Black*, *E.R.*, and *Cold Case*. Note that while Iz's version was originally part of a medley that also included "What a Wonderful World," only "Over the Rainbow" is transcribed here.

In his version, Iz plays "Over the Rainbow" with a reggae feel. A basic reggae rhythm has strums on the eighth-note offbeats (below, left). But many players (including Iz, in this case) double up on their rhythm, playing sixteenth notes on the offbeats (below, right). A huge part of the reggae feel also comes from the muting *between* strums. To do this, play a bouncy strum, then quickly lift your fretting fingers just enough for them to mute the strings. For the eighth-note example, mute after every note; for the sixteenth-note example, mute after the last sixteenth note of each pair.

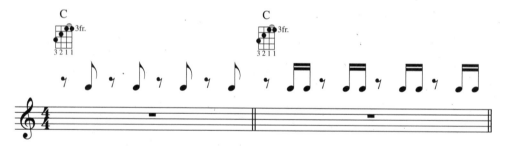

Iz strums percussively on muted strings to help drive the rhythm part. Shown with "x" noteheads, these strums are played by muting the strings with your fretting hand while strumming through those strings for a percussive "chukka" sound. In this *rhythmic notation*, strums are shown with slashed noteheads and individual bass notes are shown with standard noteheads; for individual notes, the circled number indicates which string of the chord you should play.

Intro:

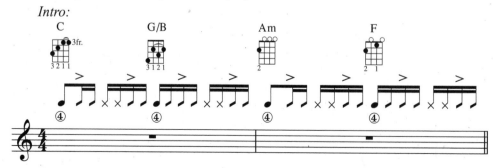

Don't get too caught up in playing the song exactly as shown in the notation. Music is about sound, and the printed page can only show you so much. Make sure to listen closely to the provided recording to understand the nuances of how the accompaniment should sound.

TIP

Iz uses *Low G tuning* in his recording, not the standard soprano uke tuning. So if you want to sound *exactly* like he does, you'll need to re-tune your ukulele slightly. The only difference between the two tunings is that, in Low G, the G string is tuned one octave lower than in standard uke tuning. (An *octave* is the distance from one note to another of the same letter name; they sound like the same note, but one is higher.) If you want to go with Low G tuning, you may need to restring your ukulele with a heavier G string.

UKULELE STARS

ISRAEL KAMAKAWIWO'OLE was a Hawaiian musician with a strong tenor voice who often backed himself on ukulele. Iz began his career as a teenager, forming the traditional Hawaiian group The Mākaha Sons in the 1970s. In the 1990s, he began recording his own albums, and it was the stripped-down medley "Over the Rainbow/What a Wonderful World"—featuring only voice and ukulele—that made him famous. Though Iz enjoyed success during his lifetime, sadly, he passed away from a weight-related respiratory problem before his popularity peaked—a popularity brought about by several posthumous releases and the use of his signature song in several movies.

Over the Rainbow

Music by HAROLD ARLEN
Lyric by E.Y. HARBURG

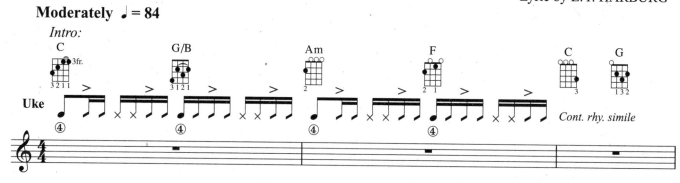

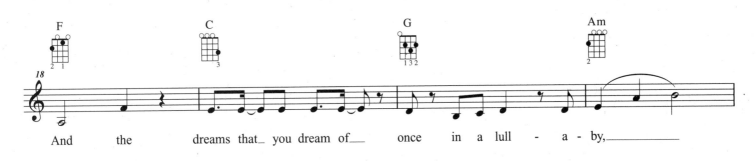

And the dreams that_ you dream of__ once in a lull - a - by,_____

oh._____ Some - where o - ver_ the rain - bow blue - birds_

fly. And the dreams that_ you dream of,__ dreams real - ly do come

% *Bridge:*

Cont. rhy. simile

true.___ Oo._____ Some-day I wish up-on_ a star, wake up where the clouds_ are far_ be -

hind me._____ Where trou-ble melts_ like lem-on drops,_ high a-bove_ the chim - ney top that's_

Ramblin' Man

Brothers and Sisters was the first complete Allman Brothers Band album recorded after guitarist Duane Allman's fatal motorcycle accident. Duane was irreplaceable, but strong tracks like "Ramblin' Man" and "Jessica" prove that guitarist/singer Dickey Betts was more than capable of shouldering a heavy load. Betts influenced the band by bringing it slightly away from the blues and more squarely into Southern rock. "Ramblin' Man" hit No. 2 on the Billboard Hot 100 and went on to become one of the band's most memorable and enduring singles. Along with Lynyrd Skynyrd's "Sweet Home Alabama," no other song embodies the Southern rock genre more than this one.

The opening lick starts up at the 10th fret and slides all the way down the fretboard. Try the fingering below, in which your 1st finger slides down from position to position on the top two strings. Once you reach the 2nd fret, you can leave your hand in that position for the final two measures of the lick. Try to minimize your hand movement here; leave your index finger hovering above the top three strings at the 1st fret, and you may even find it easier to just lay that finger down across those three strings to barre at the 2nd fret for the final *dyad* of the line.

DEFINITION

Two notes played simultaneously are called a **dyad**. You need three notes for a complete chord, but dyads can sometimes imply full chords, depending on the context.

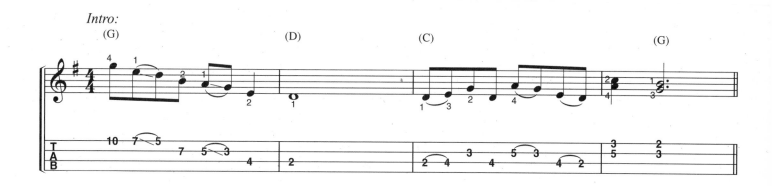

At the end of the song, starting in measure 74, dueling electric guitars play a repeating figure that's been arranged here for one ukulele. Slide into the first dyad by barring across the 2nd and 3rd strings with your 1st finger. One of the trickiest parts of this line is the set of quarter-note triplets in the next measure, which are three notes of equal duration crammed into the space of two quarter notes. In the final measure, hold down the 10th fret of the 1st string with your 4th finger and the 7th fret of the 2nd string with your 1st finger. Then, simply slide this formation down two frets before shifting up two frets to where you started. Listen carefully to the provided recording to hear how this sounds. You might find it helpful to loop this section using the TNT software.

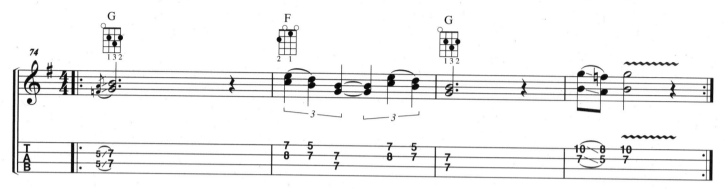

 **FUN FACT**

The original *Brothers and Sisters* album cover featured Vaylor Trucks, the son of drummer Butch Trucks, on the front cover and Brittany Oakley, the daughter of bassist Berry Oakley, on the back cover.

Ramblin' Man

Words and Music by
FORREST RICHARD BETTS

Moderately fast ♩ = 182

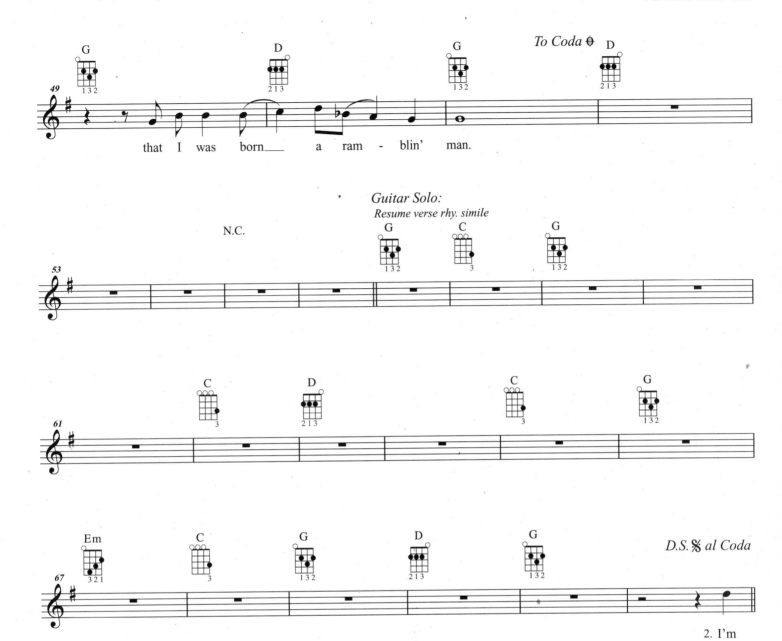

Sister Golden Hair

"Sister Golden Hair" topped the Billboard Hot 100 chart in 1975 and was the band America's second No. 1 single, after "A Horse with No Name." Released on their fifth album, *Hearts*, "Sister Golden Hair" was penned by Gerry Beckley. It was common in the band for the person who wrote the song to sing it, and this was the case with "Sister Golden Hair"—Beckley sang the lead vocal while the band's other singer-songwriters (Dewey Bunnell and Dan Peek) backed him up with harmonies.

Play the suggested strumming pattern for the rhythm part using your index finger to strum over the neck of the ukulele. (Remember: ⊓ means down-stroke, and ∨ means up-stroke.) As you can see, the pattern has consecutive down-strokes and up-strokes, which may make you want to pause between strums and thereby break the steady rhythm. Instead, keep your strumming arm moving up and down in a constant motion, often called *pendulum strumming*. Connect with the strings for every down- or up-stroke indicated, and strum through the air whenever a strum isn't indicated.

DEFINITION

Pendulum strumming gets its name from the way your arm moves when using this technique. Just as a pendulum constantly moves back and forth, your strumming arm constantly moves up and down. Simply keep your arm moving, and strum through the air for any down- or up-strokes that you don't want to sound. This avoids breaks in the rhythm that can occur by pausing at the top or bottom of a strum.

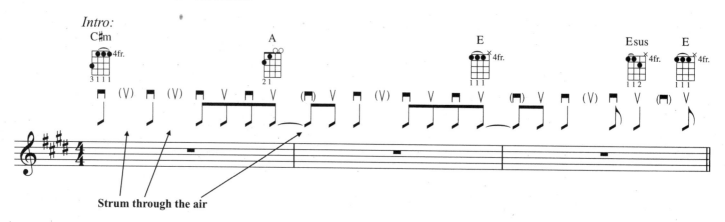

Strum through the air

On the original recording, there's an electric guitar lead played with a slide that has been adapted for ukulele in the arrangement. Since the ukulele doesn't have the sustain of an electric guitar, the held notes have been thickened with an added note or two, creating small chords. To give these even more character, each chord is quickly arpeggiated. (For more on arpeggios, see the performance notes for "Creep.") Listen carefully to the provided recording to hear how the arpeggios should sound. In the transcription, they're shown with a squiggly line to the left of the notes and TAB.

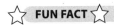 **FUN FACT**

"Sister Golden Hair" features an accidental lyric revision courtesy of Jackson Browne, who toured with America and would sing songs with the band backstage. Gerry Beckley had written the line, "Will you meet me in the middle, will you meet me in VA," but Browne mis-heard the abbreviation for "Virginia" (VA) as "the air," and sang it that way. Beckley liked it better and changed the lyric to "will you meet me in the air."

Sister Golden Hair

Words and Music by
GERRY BECKLEY

Soul Man

Key Thoughts

"Soul Man" was vocal duo Sam & Dave's biggest hit—a track that charged up to No. 2 on the Billboard Hot 100 and topped the R&B Singles chart. Released on the Stax record label, the song was written by an in-house songwriting team of Isaac Hayes and David Porter. "Soul Man" had a second wind when John Belushi and Dan Aykroyd included a version in their 1980 cult-favorite movie, *The Blues Brothers.*

Take Note

Guitarist Steve Cropper is known for his sliding 6th licks, and the opening of "Soul Man" is the definitive example. The sixteenth notes and triplet in the intro make this section look more complicated than it really is; Cropper is merely sliding a simple shape up and down the fretboard. These shapes translate easily to ukulele, and in the following example, the stripped-down shapes are shown directly beneath each of the opening four measures. Notice how they're all fingered exactly the same way, with your middle finger on the 3rd string and your ring finger on the 1st string. Practice sliding between the shapes on the second line until you're comfortable moving them around, then try it in rhythm, as shown on the top line. Notice that, when you're moving between the G and F shapes, you'll have to use hammer-ons and pull-offs; it's hard to slide to and from the open strings.

Once the song kicks into gear, Cropper plays a melodic line with three-note chord shapes. He plays this up the neck on his guitar, which translates well to open position on the ukulele. This happens pretty quickly, so listen to the provided recording to get the feel of it (and remember that you can slow it down and loop sections if you need to).

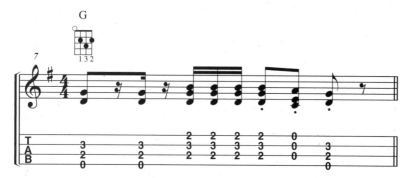

When the song changes keys in measure 31, Cropper moves his sliding 6th shape to follow the new chords. Use the same fingering here that you used in the opening section, but, unlike before, you can slide between all of these shapes, since none of them use open strings.

The outro chorus rhythm pattern mirrors the earlier verse patterns, except that we're now in a higher key: Ab. This makes the chordal pattern a little trickier to play, but if you barre across the top three strings with your index finger, the pattern is much easier. This means you'll barre at the 3rd fret for the first set of chords, adding your middle finger on the 4th fret of the 2nd string. After that, it's an easy move to slide your barred index finger down two frets to the 1st fret. Then, slide it back up to the 3rd fret and add your middle finger to finish off the figure.

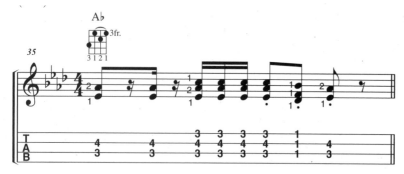

DEFINITION

An **interval** is the distance between two notes, such as the sliding 6ths in the intro of "Soul Man." To determine the size of an interval, count the notes up a scale, so the starting note is 1, the next note is 2, and so on. The interval between the first and second notes is a 2nd. When you reach the 6th note, the interval between that note and the first note is a 6th. It's important to remember that *both* notes—the starting note *and* the ending note—are included in your count.

☆ **FUN FACT** ☆

The Stax Records house band played behind Sam & Dave on "Soul Man." Featuring Booker T. Jones on keyboards, Steve Cropper on guitar, Duck Dunn on bass, and Al Jackson, Jr. on drums, the group laid down the music behind a host of other hits on the Stax label, including tracks by Otis Redding, Wilson Pickett, Albert King, and others. Also known as Booker T & the MG's, they were a successful band in their own right, recording classic songs like "Green Onions."

Soul Man

Words and Music by
ISAAC HAYES and DAVID PORTER

Verse 2:
Got what I got the hard way.
And I'll make it better each and every day.
So, honey, now, don't you fret, heh,
'Cause you ain't seen a-nothin' yet.
(To Chorus:)

Verse 3:
I was brought up on a side street.
Listen, now, I learned to love before I could eat.
I was educated at Woodstock.
When I start lovin', oh, I can't stop.
(To Chorus:)

Stairway to Heaven

Key Thoughts

"Stairway to Heaven" is arguably the most popular rock song of all time, omnipresent on classic radio playlists and in the guitar-testing section of music stores. Included on Led Zeppelin's untitled fourth album, the song was reportedly requested more than any other song on FM radio, even though it was not released as a single.

Take Note

In the original recording, the opening of "Stairway to Heaven" is played fingerstyle on an acoustic guitar, so it translates well to ukulele. In general, play the down-stemmed notes with your thumb and the up-stemmed notes with your index, middle, and ring fingers. Suggested fingerings are shown between the notation and tablature: *p* = thumb, *i* = index, *m* = middle, and *a* = ring. (For more on picking-hand fingerings, see the lesson for "If You Could Read My Mind" in this book)

At measure 41, Jimmy Page starts strumming chords. You could grab a pick for this section, but a pick might be too much for the ukulele, so strumming with your index finger tends to work best. Notice that any doubled notes played on different strings are shown as just one note in the notation; that's why you sometimes see three notes in the notation but four strings played in the TAB.

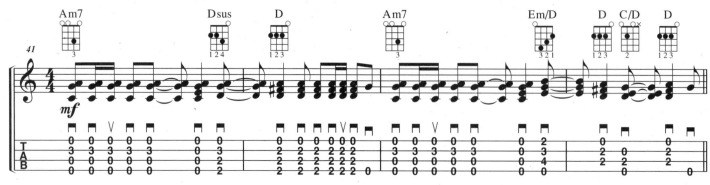

The song continues to alternate between fingerpicking and strumming sections until the interlude at measure 85, where dynamic strumming takes us to the end.

DEFINITION

Slash chords have a bass note that is not the *root note*. The chord symbols show the chord name followed by a slash and the bass note. Slash chords are stated as the chord's name "over" the bass note; for instance, the C/D chord in "Stairway to Heaven" is called "C over D."

UKULELE STARS

JAKE SHIMABUKURO is a modern-day ukulele virtuoso who gained fame on YouTube by playing complicated uke arrangements of popular songs, including Led Zeppelin's "Going to California." Shimabukuro began playing guitar at the age of four and performed in a number of contemporary Hawaiian groups, but it was his YouTube videos—especially his virtuosic rendition of The Beatles' "While My Guitar Gently Weeps"—that brought him international attention. Shimabukuro has gone on to tour and record with artists such as Jimmy Buffett, Ziggy Marley, and Béla Fleck, and continues to play uke arrangements of classic songs along with original material.

FUN FACT

Before the Yardbirds and Led Zeppelin, Jimmy Page was a prolific session guitarist, and he played on many hits by other groups throughout the '60s. While the credits are somewhat contentious, and Page, himself, claims he doesn't remember everything he contributed to, he reportedly played fuzz guitar on Donovan's "Mellow Yellow" and rhythm guitar on Them's rendition of "Baby Please Don't Go." He also reportedly played on The Kinks' debut record and even The Who song "I Can't Explain."

Stairway to Heaven

Words and Music by
JIMMY PAGE and ROBERT PLANT

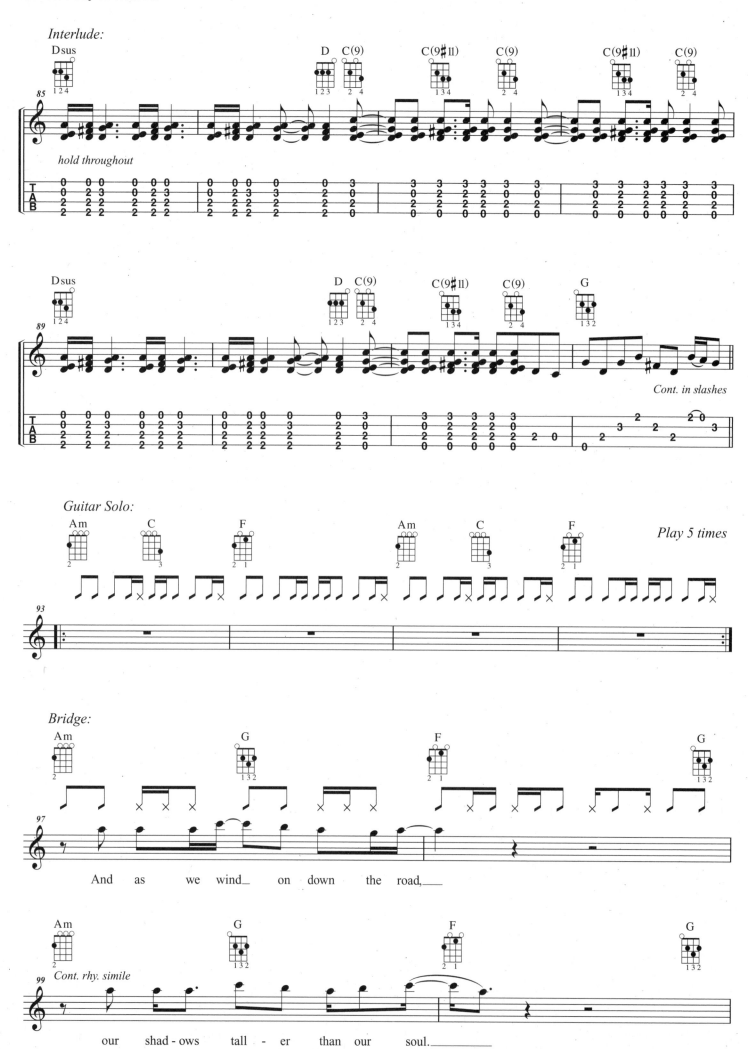

When all are one__ and one is all,_____

to be a rock__ and not to roll._____

And she's buy - ing a stair - way__ to heav - en.__

Take It Easy

 Key Thoughts

"Take It Easy" introduced Eagles to the world, and it remained a signature song throughout the band's long and successful career. The lead-off track to their 1972 self-titled debut record, "Take It Easy" was also released as a single and climbed to No. 12 on the Billboard Hot 100 chart. Sung by Glenn Frey, the song features lead guitar and banjo by Bernie Leadon.

 Take Note

The rhythm part is a driving strum pattern throughout the song. The "x" noteheads in the pattern represent partial chord strums, *not* dampened strings (which are also often notated with "x" noteheads). These strums happen most often in the transition between chords as the fret-hand fingers move to a new chord. Strumming the open strings of partial chord shapes between chords isn't that noticeable, and it's a great trick for allowing more time to get your fingers into place for the next chord. If you listen carefully to the provided recording, you'll hear these "x"s sometimes played as a complete chord, sometimes a partial chord, and sometimes the open strings are strummed. This isn't an exact science; the main point is to get the feel and know that occasionally strumming the open strings while changing chords sounds fine.

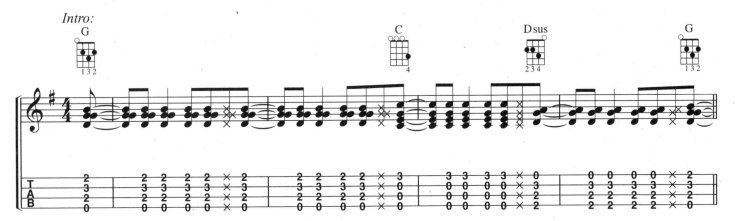

Notice that several variations occur when sections are repeated. In the verse, play a C in the fourth measure, but replace that C with an Am chord the last time you play that section (as shown in parentheses). In the second measure of the chorus, hold the Em chord the first time, but play a D chord the second and third times, as noted.

While "Take It Easy" isn't one of the more complicated songs in this book, following along with all the repeats and *codas* in the notation can prove challenging. Here's how to follow along with the music.

- Start at the beginning of the song and play to the first ending. Once you're finished with the first ending, you'll see the first few lyrics for the second verse, and a repeat that takes you back to the measure 11 for verse 2.

- Play the verse and chorus again, but this time skip over the first ending and play the second ending, which is only one measure long. The ***D.S. 𝄋 al Coda I*** at the end of this measure tells you to go back to the 𝄋 at measure 11 and play until directed to ***Coda I***. Once again, you'll be at the beginning of the verse, but this verse is actually an instrumental.

- After you play the instrumental verse and most of the chorus starting from the D.S., the ***To Coda I*** indication at the end of measure 25 means to jump to ***Coda I***, which is to measure 38. ***Coda I*** is only one bar long, and ***D.S. 𝄋 al Coda II*** means to go back again to the 𝄋 and play until directed to ***Coda II*** at the end of measure 25. Jump directly to measure 39. From here on out, it's smooth sailing—just play straight through to the end! (Whew!)

DEFINITION

Many of Western civilization's musical terms are Italian, like the terms for endings, repeats, and related directions. A **coda** is essentially a concluding section. The term **D.S.** is the abbreviation for *dal segno*, which means "from the sign." A similar direction is **D.C.**, the abbreviation for *da capo*, meaning "from the beginning," which tells you to go back to the very beginning of a song. In popular music, these directions are often used to streamline long pieces into fewer pages.

☆ FUN FACT ☆

Jackson Browne co-wrote "Take It Easy" with Glenn Frey; they were neighbors at the time. Frey had heard an early version of a tune that Browne was working on and Frey liked it so much that he added some lyrics and convinced Browne to let him use it with Eagles. Browne later released his own version on his second album, *For Everyman*

Take It Easy

Words and Music by
JACKSON BROWNE
and GLENN FREY

Moderately ♩ = 138

Intro:

*Unison A notes played
on 1st and 2nd strings
(see TAB).

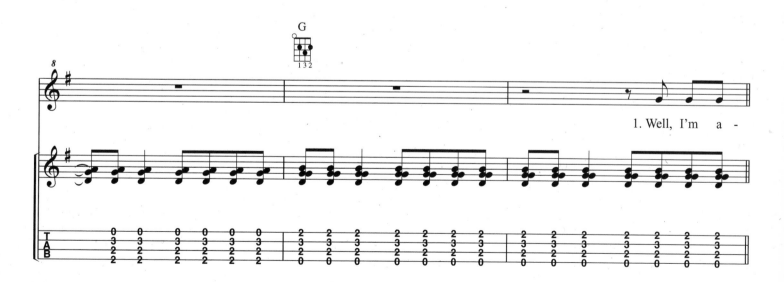

1. Well, I'm a -

%⟡ *Verse:*

run-nin' down the road, try'n' to loos-en my load,__ I got sev - en wom-en on my__ mind: four__

2.3. *See additional lyrics*
4. *Instrumental*

*last time substitute Am for C.

Cont. rhy. simile

__ that wan - na own me, two__ that wan - na stone me, one__ says she's a friend__ of mine.__

Chorus:

1.3. Take it__ eas - y, take it__ eas -
2. *See additional lyrics*

*2nd & 3rd times play D.

y. Don't let the

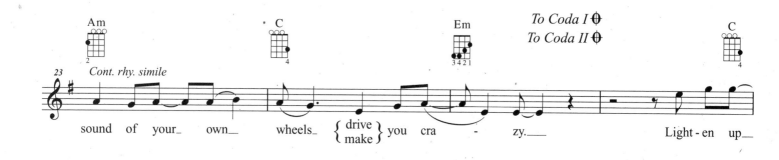

Am   C   Em   To Coda I
                                            To Coda II   C

sound of your_ own_ wheels_ { drive / make } you cra - zy.__ Light-en up_

G   C   G

__ while you still can,___ don't e-ven try___ to un-der-stand,___ just find a

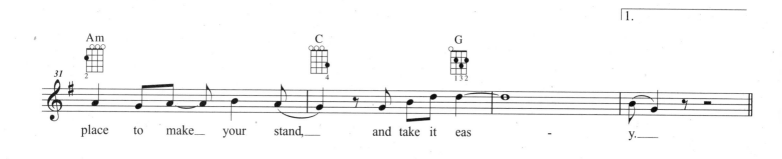

Am   C   G   1.

place to make__ your stand,___ and take it eas - y.___

2.   D.S. % al Coda I
                   (To Instrumental)

G

2. Well, I'm a _ y.___

Coda I

D.S. % al Coda II

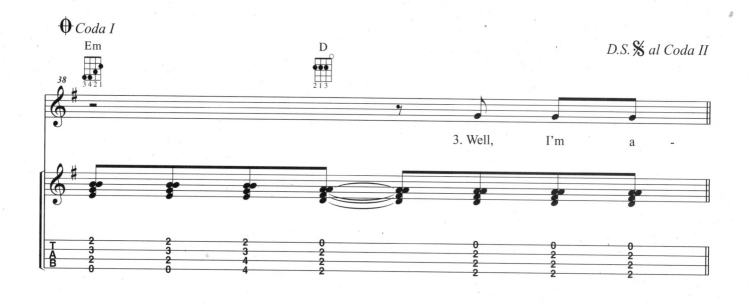

3. Well, I'm a -

Coda II

Come on,__ ba - by, don't say__ may -

be. I__ got-ta know if your__ sweet love__ is gon - na save_____ me.__

Outro:

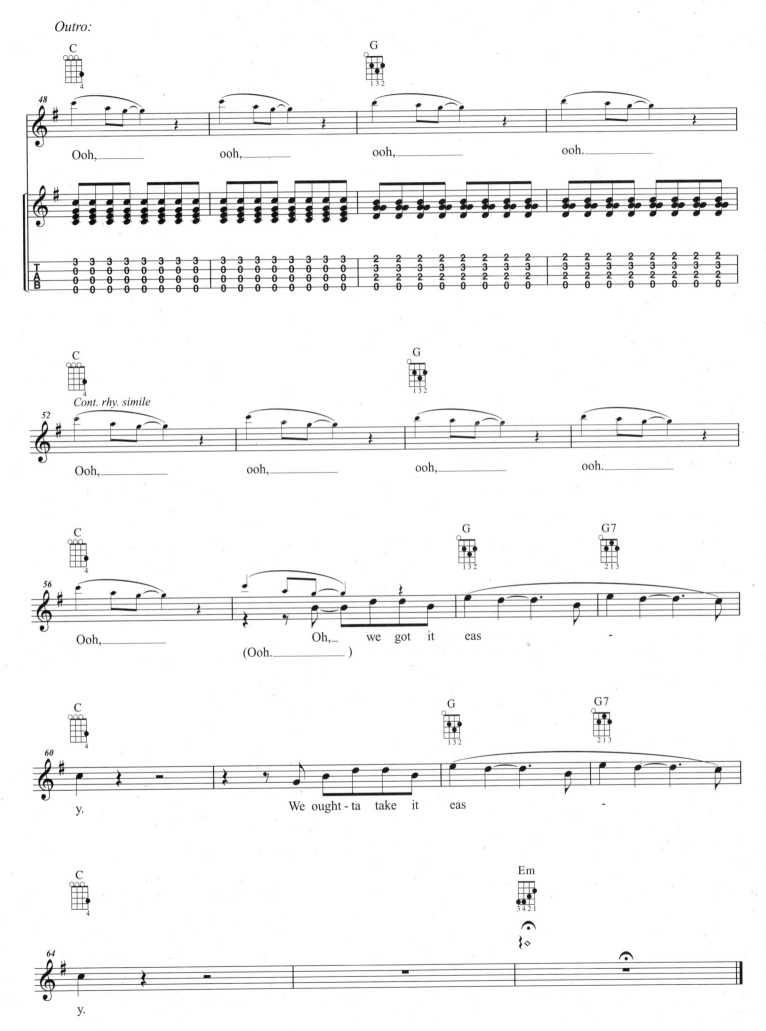

Sunshine of Your Love

Key Thoughts

Cream produced so many classic hits that it's hard to believe they were only around for a few years. Their biggest hit of all, "Sunshine of Your Love," melded passionate vocals, a heavy guitar and bass riff, and a psychedelic tom-tom drum pattern into a radio-friendly package that climbed all the way to No. 5 on the Billboard Hot 100.

Take Note

The main riff in "Sunshine of Your Love" provides the foundation for the intro and most of the verse. The lick starts off as a single-note line, but the first four notes morph into full chords by the third time through, adding extra heft. When you're playing just single notes, the volume might be a bit too low, so one way to add punch is to mute a string on either side of the fretted note, and play through that string as well. The muted string won't sound a note, but you'll hear some added punch from the attack. It's easiest to roll your fretting finger down and mute the next-highest string (the string closer to the floor), but you can also include other strings by muting lower ones with your other fingers—or the tips of your fretting fingers—for even more punch.

On the second-to-last note of each two-measure riff, play the *vibrato* by moving your fretting finger quickly up and down the string within the fret to add texture. To see how this vibrato should sound, listen to the provided recording.

DEFINITION

Vibrato is a slight fluctuation in pitch that musicians use to add texture to their sound. It's indicated above notation and TAB with a wavy, horizontal line over the note. On fretless string instruments like the violin and viola, vibrato is often used quite liberally, but on fretted stringed instruments like the ukulele and guitar, vibrato is used sparingly. Classical and rock musicians have differing techniques when playing vibrato on the fretted instruments. Classical players rock *between* the frets (side to side) for a subtle vibrato, while rock players push and pull the string up and down (like bending a note) for a more dramatic vibrato.

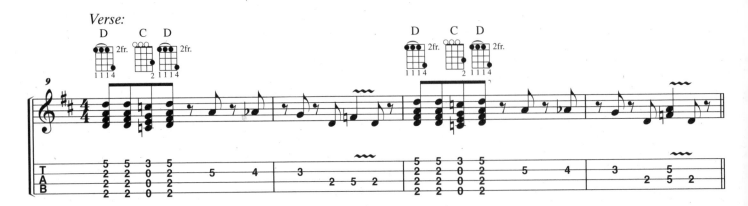

Verse:

TIP

If you have trouble playing the vibrato by barring the two notes on the 5th fret in measure 4, try fretting the notes with two fingers, such as your ring and pinky fingers.

Midway through the verse, the riff is played over F and G chords. To play this phrase, simply move the exact same shapes five frets up.

UKULELE STARS

Eric Clapton is one of the guitar world's biggest names, with a reputation that inspired an anonymous graffiti artist to spray-paint "Clapton Is God" on a London Underground wall. Likewise, **CLIFF EDWARDS** was one of the ukulele world's biggest names in the earlier part of the 20th century. Known as "Ukulele Ike," Edwards's uke strumming and three-octave vocal range helped him carve a name for himself. With a long career in Hollywood and on Broadway, he is best known for his Oscar-winning performance of "When You Wish Upon a Star" that appeared in Disney's film *Pinocchio*.

Sunshine of Your Love

Words and Music by
JACK BRUCE, PETE BROWN
and ERIC CLAPTON

Moderately ♩ = 114

Intro:

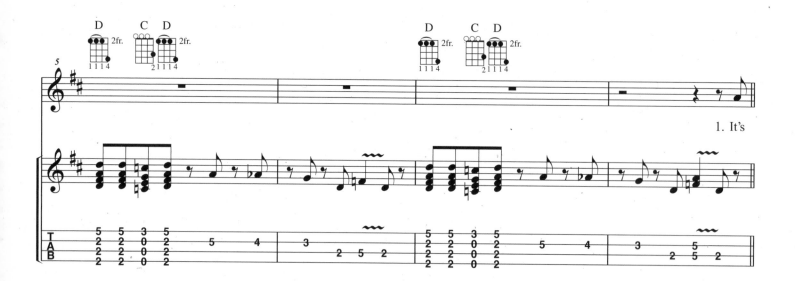

1. It's

get - ting near dawn,   when lights close their tired   eyes.
(2.4.) with you, my love,   the light shin - ing through on you.
(3.) *Guitar Solo*

I've been wait - ing so long, to be where I'm go - ing,

Cont. in notation

in the sun - shine of your love.

2. I'm love.

Cont. in notation

Tonight You Belong to Me

Key Thoughts

Lyricist Billy Rose and musician Lee David wrote "Tonight You Belong to Me" in 1926. The song has been recorded dozens of times across a variety of genres, and this ukulele arrangement is based on the version featured in Steve Martin's movie *The Jerk*. In the movie, Steve Martin and Bernadette Peters walk along the beach singing the song while Martin gently strums accompaniment on a uke.

Take Note

Don't let the large number of chords in this arrangement overwhelm you. With a little practice, you should be able to make it all the way through, but a few things can help you master the chord changes a little more quickly. First, notice how, in many places, a chord shape is simply moved up or down a fret. Even though this puts some extra chords on the page, simply shifting your hand up or down a fret is easy. Make sure to listen to the provided recording and slow it down to hear how these one-fret shifts color the sound. Here are several instances where this happens:

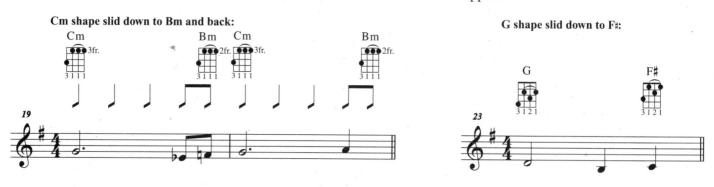

When there are multiple chord changes in a measure, you can move between the chords more easily by fretting and playing only the top three notes of each chord. The following excerpts include frames of the full chord shapes, but the notation and TAB show the changes with just the top three strings. (Make sure to play the *bottom* two strings only at the end of the first measure.)

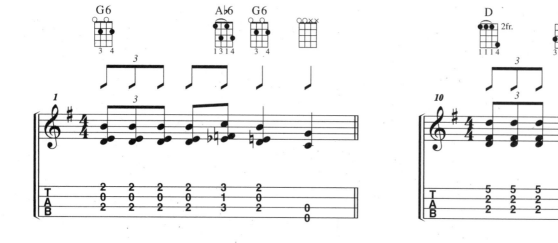

If you still have trouble grabbing all the chords, you can also simplify the arrangement. Many of the chords are "color" chords, which means they aren't absolutely needed for the song to sound good—they just enhance it. When a chord with the same letter name (the root) moves through several types of forms, often you can often get away with leaving a chord or two out. For example, when moving between G7 and G7sus, the G7sus can be omitted. The following example shows how you might simplify the first four measures of the verse, starting at measure 3. Remember that you can always put chords back in when you're ready.

know   (I know)   you be - long_____   to   some - bod-y   new_____   but to -

UKULELE STARS

Though Steve Martin is shown playing the ukulele for "Tonight You Belong to Me" in *The Jerk*, the part was actually recorded by **LYLE RITZ**. Ritz recorded two jazz ukulele records in the late 1950s, but spent much of his professional career as an accomplished bass player in Hollywood for countless jazz, rock, and pop acts, as well as film and TV soundtracks. His groundbreaking early uke recordings guaranteed him status as a jazz ukulele hero, and he continues to perform and record today.

Tonight You Belong to Me

Words and Music by
BILLY ROSE and LEE DAVID

Wild Night

Tupelo Honey was released right in the middle of Van Morrison's classic period—a time ranging roughly from 1968–1974. Released in 1971, the album features Stax-inspired R&B tracks with horns and the hit song "Wild Night," which climbed up to No. 28 on the Billboard Hot 100 chart. But "Wild Night" in its original form was nearly a completely different song. As Morrison tells it, the song "was originally a much slower number, but when we got to fooling around with it in the studio, we ended up doing it in a faster tempo. So they put it out as a single."

"Wild Night" starts with strummed Em chords, but notice how when you reach the G chord in measure 3, an embellishment is indicated in the notation and TAB. This bluesy embellishment rocks back and forth between two notes on the 3rd string. If you finger the G chord as shown in the chord frame above the notation with your 1st and 2nd fingers, that will leave your 3rd finger free to grab the E note on the 4th fret. This figure happens over every G chord in the song.

*See TAB for riff played over the G chord throughout.

In measure 5, a melodic bass line enters, arranged here for ukulele. This bass line is built from a G major pentatonic scale that starts at the 7th fret of the 3rd string. Get comfortable with this position by playing up and down the G major pentatonic scale in the following example. Once you're familiar with the scale, the bass line should fall easily under your fingers.

Two measures before the chorus, there's an electric guitar fill based on sliding 6th interval shapes. (For more on intervals, see Appendix A: Chord Theory.) The lick works just as well on ukulele. There are two 6th shapes that use notes on the 1st and 3rd strings (below, left), and they can interlock to create licks all the way up and down the fretboard. If you play the first shape with your 1st and 2nd fingers and the second one with your 3rd and 2nd fingers, the shapes slide easily into each other. Try it out with the fill (below, right). And one more thing—once you reach the 2nd fret, it's easier to pull-off to the open string than it is to slide down.

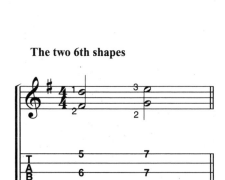

The two 6th shapes

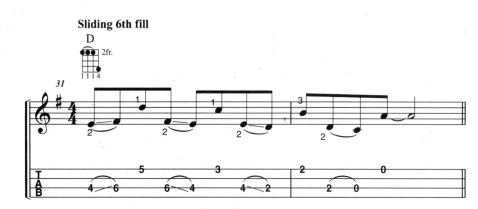

Sliding 6th fill

FUN FACT

Van Morrison recorded *Tupelo Honey* in the most live setting possible. The band would rehearse the songs in the studio and then play through a whole set in one take. Album co-producer Ted Templeman said, "(it was the) scariest thing I've ever seen. When he's got something together, he wants to put it down right away with no overdubbing."

Wild Night

Moderately fast ♩ = 148

Words and Music by
VAN MORRISON

*See TAB for riff played over the G chord throughout.

dance.   Come on___ out,   make ro - mance.___

Chord Theory

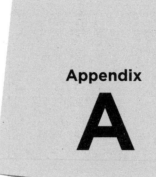

You don't have to understand the music theory of chord construction to play the songs in this book. The notation, TAB, and chord diagrams tell you everything you need to know to play the music correctly. Someday, though, you're bound to find music that doesn't give you as much information as we have, and you'll need to know at least a little bit about chords to get it right. This section should help you out in those situations, and also add some basic chops to your knowledge of music.

Intervals

Play any note on the ukulele, then play a note one fret above it. The distance between these two notes is a *half step*. Play another note followed by a note two frets above it. The distance between these notes is a *whole step* (two half steps). The distance between any two notes is referred to as an *interval*.

In the example of the C major scale on the following page, the letter names are shown above the notes, and the *scale degrees* (numbers) of the notes are written below. Notice that C is the first degree of the scale, D is the second, and so on.

The name of an interval is determined by counting the number of scale degrees from one note to the next. For example, an interval of a 3rd, starting on C, would be determined by counting up three scale degrees, or C–D–E (1–2–3). C to E is a 3rd. An interval of a 4th, starting on C, would be determined by counting up four scale degrees, or C–D–E–F (1–2–3–4). C to F is a 4th.

Intervals are not only labeled by the distance between scale degrees, but by the *quality* of the interval. An interval's quality is determined by counting the number of whole steps and half steps between the two notes of that interval. For example, C to E is a 3rd. C to E is also a *major* 3rd because there are 2 whole steps between C and E. Likewise, C to E♭ is a 3rd. C to E♭ is also a *minor* third because there are 1½ steps between C and E♭.

There are five qualities used to describe intervals: *major, minor, perfect, diminished,* and *augmented*.

Interval Qualities

Quality	Abbreviation
major	M
minor	m
perfect	P
diminished	dim or °
augmented	aug or +

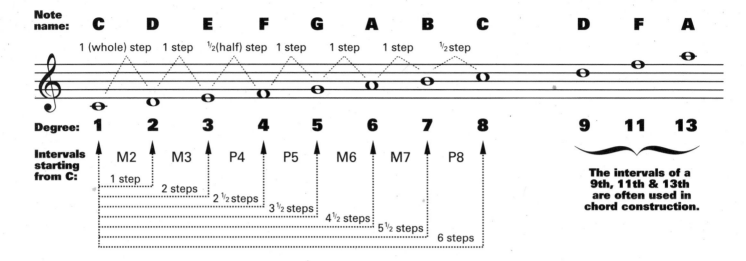

Particular intervals are associated with certain qualities. Not all qualities pertain to every type of interval, as seen in the following table.

Interval Type	Possible Qualities
2nd, 9th	major, minor, augmented
3rd, 6th, 13th	major, minor, diminished, augmented
4th, 5th, 11th	perfect, diminished, augmented
7th	major, minor, diminished

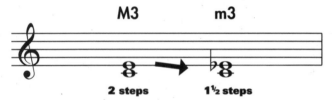

When a major interval is made smaller by a half step, it becomes a minor interval.

When a minor interval is made larger by a half step, it becomes a major interval.

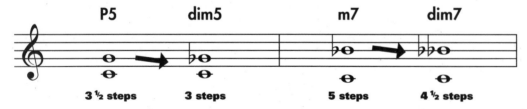

When a perfect or minor interval is made smaller by a half step, it becomes a diminished interval.

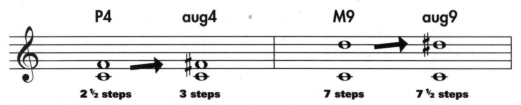

When a perfect or major interval is made larger by a half step, it becomes an augmented interval.

Following is a table of intervals starting on the note C. Notice that some intervals are labeled *enharmonic*, which means that they are written differently but sound the same (see aug2 and m3).

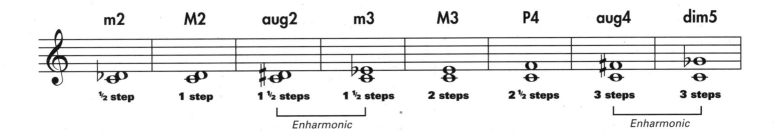

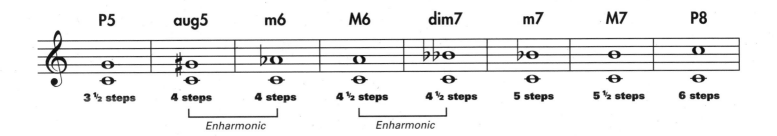

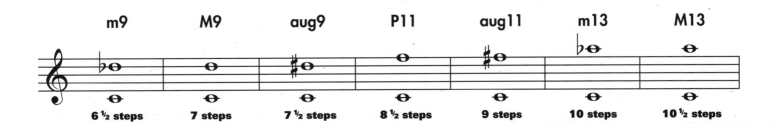

Basic Triads

Two or more notes played together are called a *chord*. Most commonly, a chord will consist of three or more notes. A three-note chord is called a *triad*. The *root* of a triad (or any other chord) is the note from which a chord is constructed. The relationship of the intervals from the root to the other notes of a chord determines the chord *type*. Triads are most frequently identified as one of four chord types: *major*, *minor*, *diminished*, and *augmented*.

Chord Types

All chord types can be identified by the intervals used to create the chord. For example, the C major triad is built beginning with C as the root, adding a major 3rd (E) and adding a perfect 5th (G). All major triads contain a root, M3, and P5.

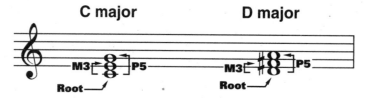

Minor triads contain a root, minor 3rd, and perfect 5th. (An easier way to build a minor triad is to simply lower the 3rd of a major triad.) All minor triads contain a root, m3, and P5.

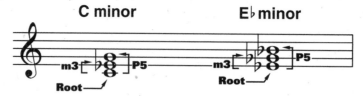

Diminished triads contain a root, minor 3rd, and diminished 5th. If the perfect 5th of a minor triad is made smaller by a half step (to become a diminished 5th), the result is a diminished triad. All diminished triads contain a root, m3, and dim5.

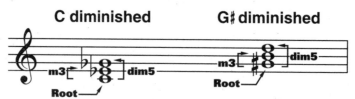

Augmented triads contain a root, major 3rd, and augmented 5th. If the perfect 5th of a major triad is made larger by a half step (to become an augmented 5th), the result is an augmented triad. All augmented triads contain a root, M3, and aug5.

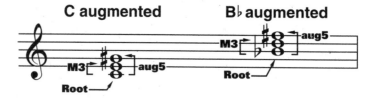

Chord Inversions

An important concept to remember about chords is that the bottom note of a chord will not always be the root. If the root of a triad, for instance, is moved above the 5th so that the 3rd is the bottom note of the chord, it is said to be in the *first inversion*. If the root and 3rd are moved above the 5th, the chord is in the *second inversion*. The number of inversions that a chord can have is related to the number of notes in the chord: a three-note chord can have two inversions, a four-note chord can have three inversions, etc.

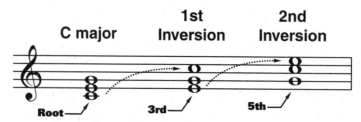

Building Chords

By using the four chord types as basic building blocks, it is possible to create a variety of chords by adding 6ths, 7ths, 9ths, 11ths, and so on. The following are examples of some of the many variations.

So far, the examples provided to illustrate intervals and chord construction have been based on C. Until you're familiar with chords, the C chord examples on the previous page can serve as a guide for building chords based on other notes. For example, to construct a G7(♭9) chord, you can first determine what intervals are contained in C7(♭9) and use the steps below to build the same chord starting on G.

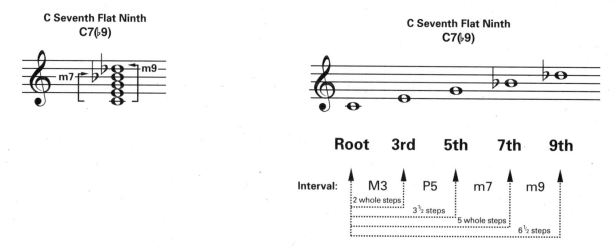

* First, determine the *root* of the chord. A chord is always named for its root, so G is the root of G7(♭9).

* Count *letter names* up from the *letter name of the root* (G) to determine the intervals of the chord. Counting three letter names up from G to B (G–A–B, 1–2–3) is a 3rd, G to D (G–A–B–C–D) is a 5th, G to F is a 7th, and G to A is a 9th.

* Determine the *quality* of the intervals by counting half steps and whole steps up from the root. G to B (2 whole steps) is a major 3rd, G to D (3½ steps) is a perfect 5th, G to F (5 whole steps) is a minor 7th, and G to A♭ (6½ steps) is a minor 9th.

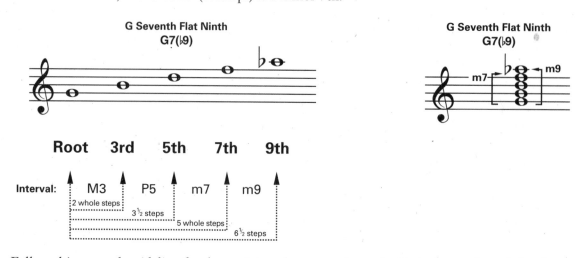

Follow this general guideline for determining the notes of any chord. As intervals and chord construction become more familiar to you, you'll be able to create original fingerings on the ukulele. Don't be afraid to experiment!

The Circle of Fifths

The *circle of fifths* will help to clarify which chords are enharmonic equivalents (yes, chords can be written enharmonically as well as notes). The circle of fifths also serves as a quick reference guide to the relationship of the keys and how key signatures can be figured out in a logical manner. Moving clockwise (up a P5) provides all of the sharp keys by progressively adding one sharp to the key signature. Moving counter-clockwise (down a P5) provides the flat keys by progressively adding one flat to the key signature.

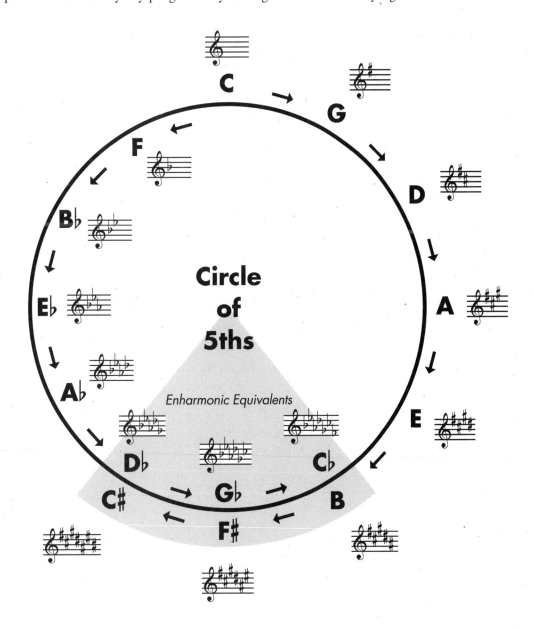

Chord Symbol Variations

Chord symbols are a form of musical shorthand that provide you with as much information about a chord as quickly as possible. The intent of using chord symbols is to convey enough information to recognize the chord, yet not so much as to confuse the meaning of the symbol. Chord symbols are not universally standardized and are written in many different ways—some are easy to understand, others are confusing. To illustrate this point, following is a list of some of the variations copyists, composers, and arrangers have created for the more common chord symbols.

C	Csus	C(♭5)	C(add9)	C5	Cm
C major	Csus4	C-5	C(9)	C(no3)	Cmin
Cmaj	C(addF)	C(5-)	C(add2)	C(omit3)	Cmi
CM	C4	C(♯4)	C(+9)		C-
			C(+D)		

C+	C°	C6	C6/9	Cm6/9	Cm6
C+5	Cdim	Cmaj6	C6(add9)	C-6/9	C-6
Caug	Cdim7	C(addA)	C6(addD)	Cm6(+9)	Cm(addA)
Caug5	C7dim	C(A)	C9(no7)	Cm6(add9)	Cm(+6)
C(♯5)			C9/6	Cm6(+D)	

C7	C7sus	Cm7	Cm7(♭5)	C7+	C7(♭5)
C(addB♭)	C7sus4	Cmi7	Cmi7-5	C7+5	C7-5
C7̶	Csus7	Cmin7	C-7(5-)	C7aug	C7(5-)
C(-7)	C7(+4)	C-7	Cø	C7aug5	C7̶-5
C(+7)		C7mi	C ½dim	C7(♯5)	C7(♯4)

Cmaj7	Cmaj7(♭5)	Cm(maj7)	C7(♭9)	C7(♯9)	C7+(♭9)
Cma7	Cmaj7(-5)	C-maj7	C7(-9)	C7(+9)	Caug7-9
C7̶	C7̶(-5)	C-7̶	C9♭	C9♯	C+7(♭9)
CΔ	CΔ(♭5)	Cmi7̶	C9-	C9+	C+9♭
CΔ7					C7+(-9)

Cm9	C9	C9+	C9(♭5)	Cmaj9	C9(♯11)
Cm7(9)	C$^9_7$	C9(+5)	C9(-5)	C7̶(9)	C9(+11)
Cm7(+9)	C7add9	Caug9	C7$^9_{-5}$	C7̶(+9)	C(♯11)
C-9	C7(addD)	C(♯9♯5)	C9(5♭)	C9(maj7)	C11+
Cmi7(9+)	C7(+9)	C+9		C9̶	C11♯

Cm9(maj7)	C11	Cm11	C13	C13(♭9)	C13($^{♭9}_{♭5}$)
C-9(♯7)	C9(11)	C-11	C9addA	C13(-9)	C13(-9-5)
C(-9)7̶	C9addF	Cm(♭11)	C9(6)	C$^{13}_{♭9}$	C(♭9♭5)addA
Cmi9(♯7)	C9+11	Cmi7$^{11}_9$	C7addA	C(♭9)addA	
	C7$^9_{11}$	C-7($^9_{11}$)	C7+A		

Reading Chord Frames

Ukulele chord frames are diagrams that show the fingering and position of a particular chord on the neck of the ukulele. Vertical lines represent the strings, and horizontal lines represent the frets. Dots on the diagram show exactly where to place the fingers, and corresponding numbers at the bottom of the frame tell which fingers to use.

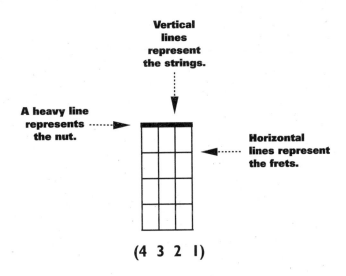

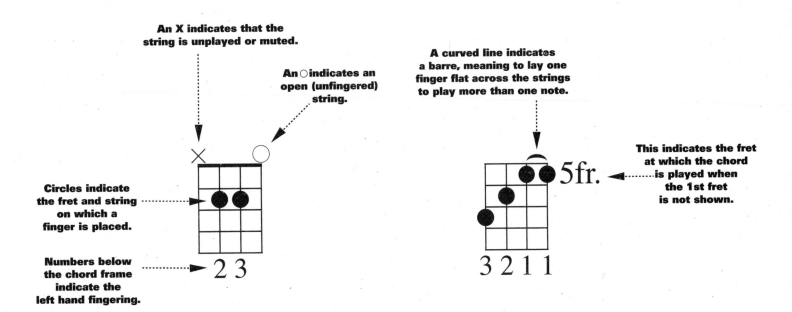

Ukulele
Fingerboard Chart

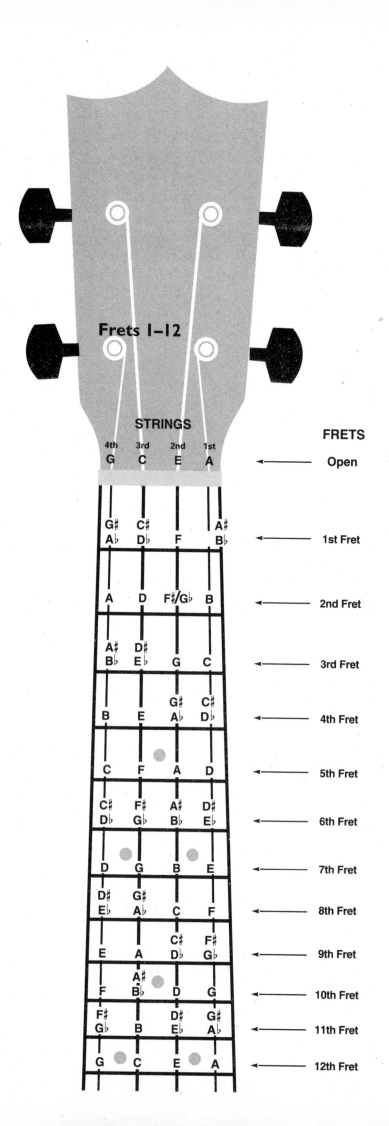

Frets 1–12

STRINGS

4th	3rd	2nd	1st	FRETS
G	C	E	A	Open
G# A♭	C# D♭	F	A# B♭	1st Fret
A	D	F#/G♭	B	2nd Fret
A# B♭	D# E♭	G	C	3rd Fret
B	E	G# A♭	C# D♭	4th Fret
C	F	A	D	5th Fret
C# D♭	F# G♭	A# B♭	D# E♭	6th Fret
D	G	B	E	7th Fret
D# E♭	G# A♭	C	F	8th Fret
E	A	C# D♭	F# G♭	9th Fret
F	A# B♭	D	G	10th Fret
F# G♭	B	D# E♭	G# A♭	11th Fret
G	C	E	A	12th Fret

Ukulele Chord Dictionary

A CHORDS

A
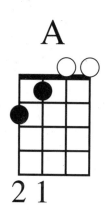
2 1

A
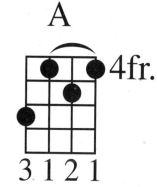
4fr.
3 1 2 1

Amaj7
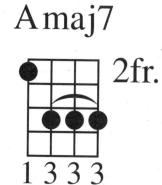
2fr.
1 3 3 3

A6
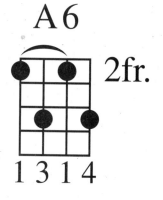
2fr.
1 3 1 4

Am
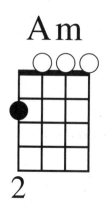
2

Am
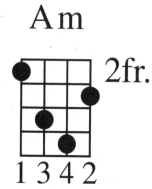
2fr.
1 3 4 2

Am7

Am6

2   3

A7
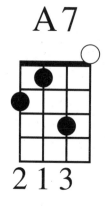
2 1 3

A7
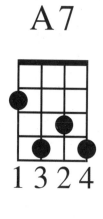
1 3 2 4

A9
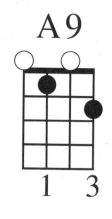
1   3

A13

1 2 3

Asus
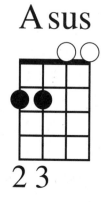
2 3

A7sus
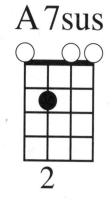
2

Adim7
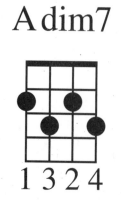
1 3 2 4

A+

3 1 2

B♭ (A♯) CHORDS

B♭
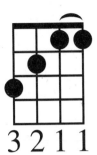
3 2 1 1

B♭
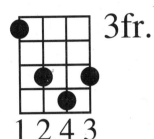
3fr.
1 2 4 3

B♭maj7
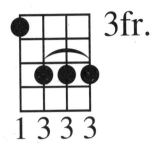
3fr.
1 3 3 3

B♭6
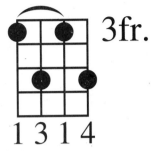
3fr.
1 3 1 4

B♭m
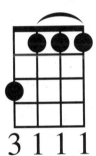
3 1 1 1

B♭m

3fr.
1 3 4 2

B♭m7
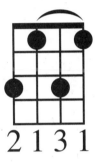
1 1 1 1

B♭m6
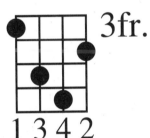
2 1 3 1

B♭7
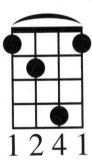
1 2 4 1

B♭7
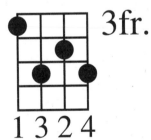
3fr.
1 3 2 4

B♭9
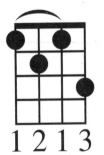
1 2 1 3

B♭13
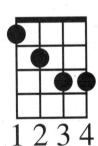
1 2 3 4

B♭sus
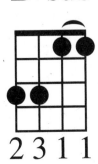
2 3 1 1

B♭7sus

1 3 4 1

B♭dim7

1 3 2 4

B♭+
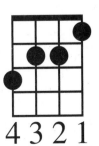
4 3 2 1

*B♭ and A♯ are two names for the same note.

B CHORDS

B

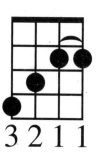

3 2 1 1

B

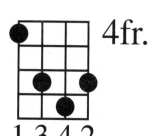

4fr.

1 3 4 2

B maj7

4 3 2 1

B 6

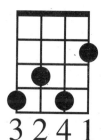

3 2 4 1

B m

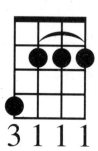

3 1 1 1

B m

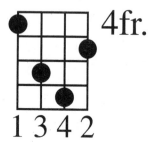

4fr.

1 3 4 2

B m7

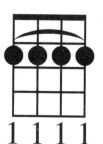

1 1 1 1

B m6

2 1 3 1

B 7

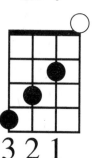

3 2 1

B 7

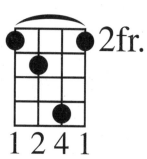

2fr.

1 2 4 1

B 9

1 2 1 3

B 13

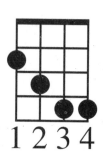

1 2 3 4

B sus

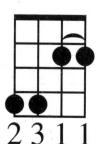

2 3 1 1

B 7sus

1 3 1 1

B dim7

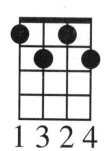

1 3 2 4

B +

4 3 2 1

C CHORDS

C
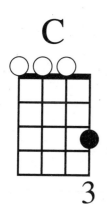
3

C
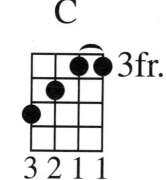
3fr.
3 2 1 1

Cmaj7
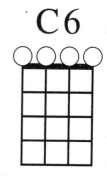
2

C6

Cm
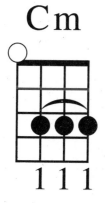
1 1 1

Cm
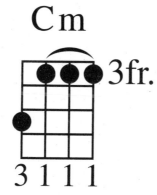
3fr.
3 1 1 1

Cm7
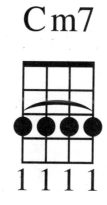
1 1 1 1

Cm6

1 3 3 3

C7
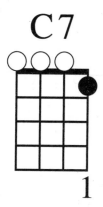
1

C7
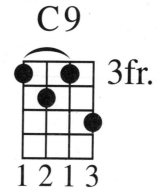
1 2 1 1

C9
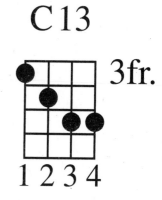
3fr.
1 2 1 3

C13
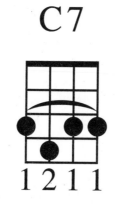
3fr.
1 2 3 4

Csus
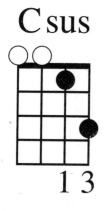
1 3

C7sus
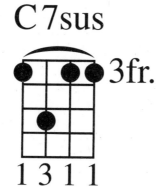
3fr.
1 3 1 1

Cdim7
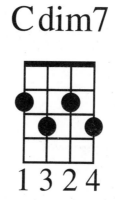
1 3 2 4

C+
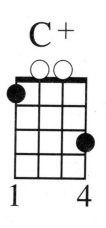
1 4

C♯ (D♭) CHORDS

C♯

1 1 1 3

C♯
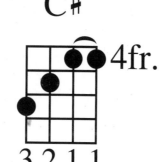
4fr.
3 2 1 1

C♯maj7

1 1 1 3

C♯6
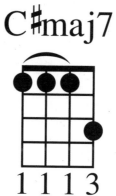
1 1 1 1

C♯m
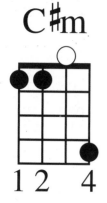
1 2   4

C♯m
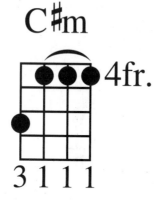
4fr.
3 1 1 1

C♯m7
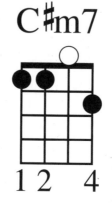
1 2   4

C♯m6
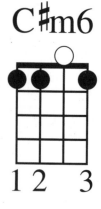
1 2   3

C♯7

1 1 1 2

C♯7
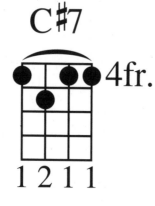
4fr.
1 2 1 1

C♯9
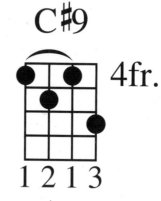
4fr.
1 2 1 3

C♯13
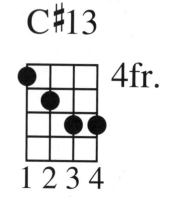
4fr.
1 2 3 4

C♯sus
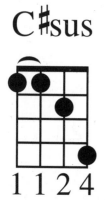
1 1 2 4

C♯7sus
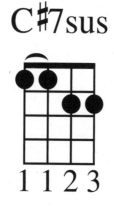
1 1 2 3

C♯dim7
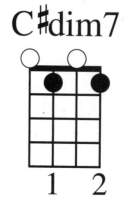
1   2

C♯+
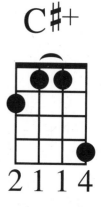
2 1 1 4

*C♯ and D♭ are two names for the same note.

D CHORDS

D

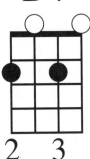

1 1 2

D

5fr.

3 2 1 1

Dmaj7

1 1 1 3

D6

1 1 1 1

Dm

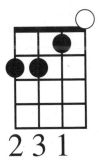

2 3 1

Dm

5fr.

3 1 1 1

Dm7

2 3 1 4

Dm6

2 3 1 4

D7

2   3

D7

1 1 1 2

D9

1 3 1 2

D13

5fr.

1 2 3 3

Dsus

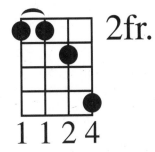

2fr.

1 1 2 4

D7sus

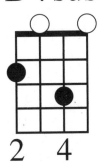

2   4

Ddim7

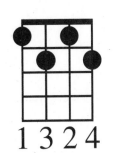

1 3 2 4

D+

4 2 3 1

E♭ (D♯) CHORDS

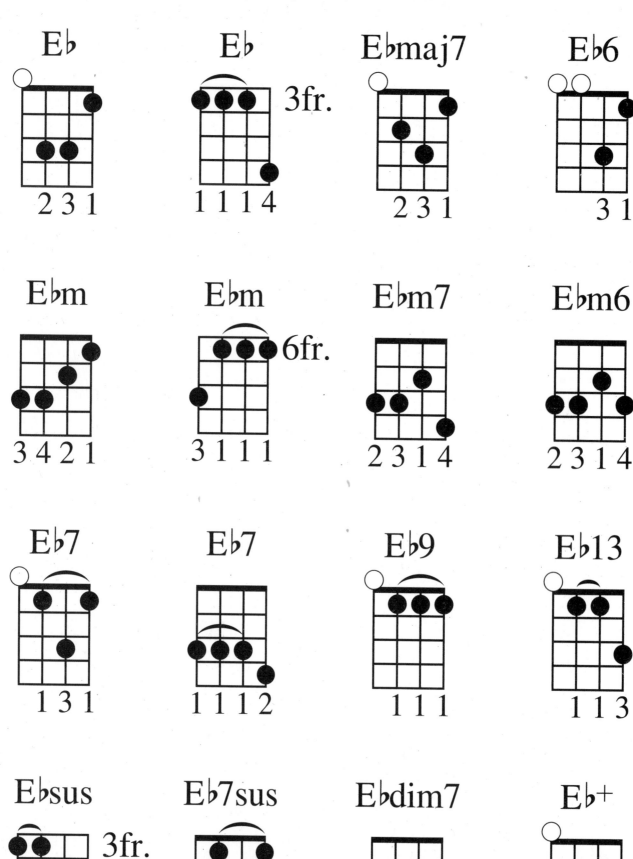

*E♭ and D♯ are two names for the same note.

E CHORDS

E

2 2 3 1

E
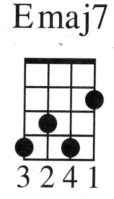
4fr.
1 1 1 4

Emaj7
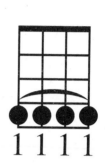
3 2 4 1

E6
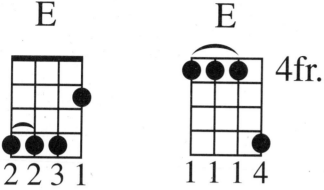
1 1 1 1

Em
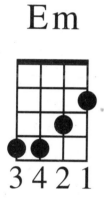
3 4 2 1

Em
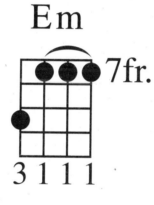
7fr.
3 1 1 1

Em7
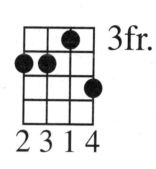
3fr.
2 3 1 4

Em6

2 3 1 4

E7
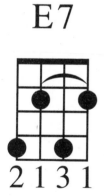
2 1 3 1

E7
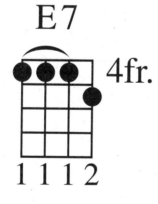
4fr.
1 1 1 2

E9

1 3 3 3

E13

1 2 2 4

Esus
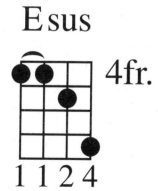
4fr.
1 1 2 4

E7sus
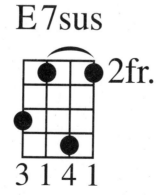
2fr.
3 1 4 1

Edim7
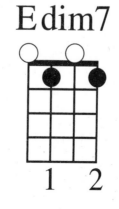
1   2

E+
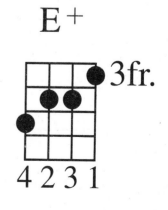
3fr.
4 2 3 1

F CHORDS

F

2   1

F
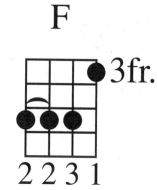
3fr.
2 2 3 1

Fmaj7
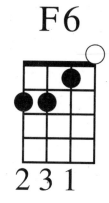
2

F6
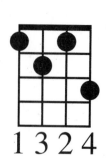
2 3 1

Fm
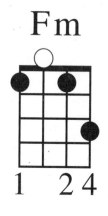
1   2 4

Fm
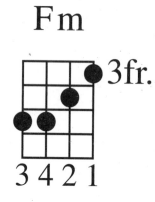
3fr.
3 4 2 1

Fm7
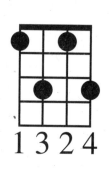
1 3 2 4

Fm6

1 3 2 4

F7
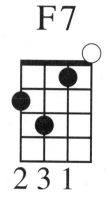
2 3 1

F7
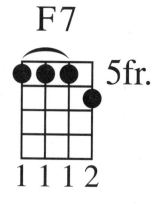
5fr.
1 1 1 2

F9
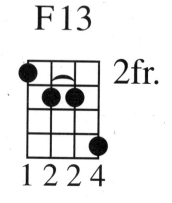
1 3 3 3

F13

2fr.
1 2 2 4

Fsus
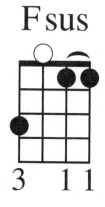
3   1 1

F7sus
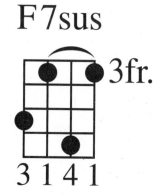
3fr.
3 1 4 1

Fdim7
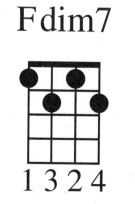
1 3 2 4

F+
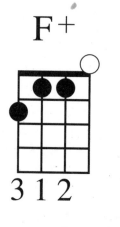
3 1 2

F♯ (G♭) CHORDS

F♯
3 1 2 1

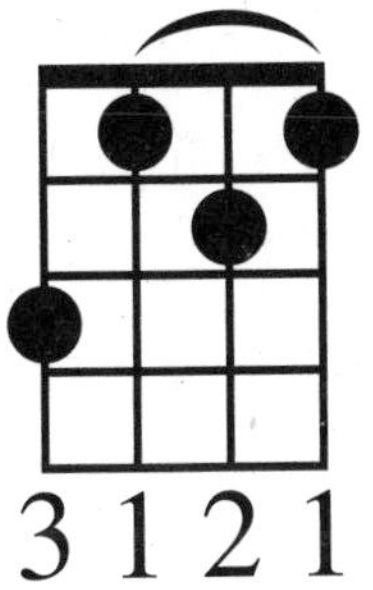

F♯
3 1 2 4

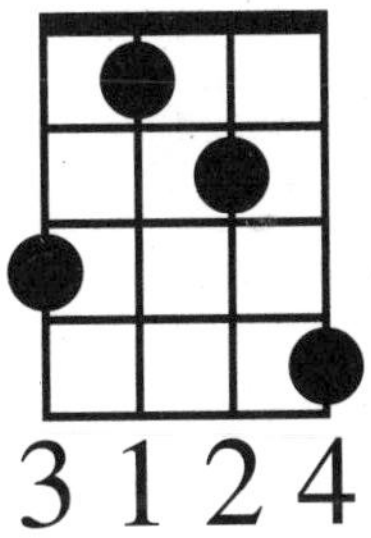

F♯maj7
3 1 1 1

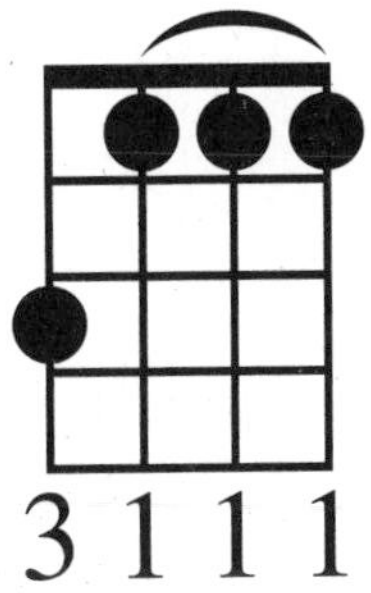

F♯6
3 4 2 1

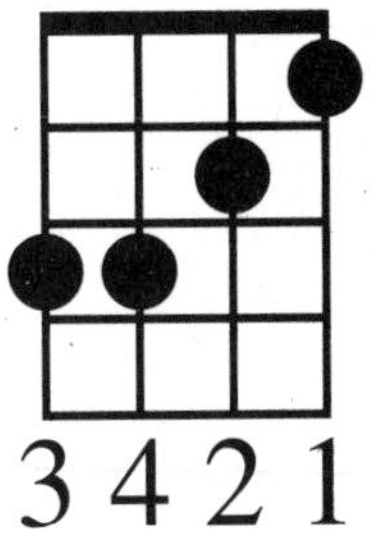

F♯m
2 1 3

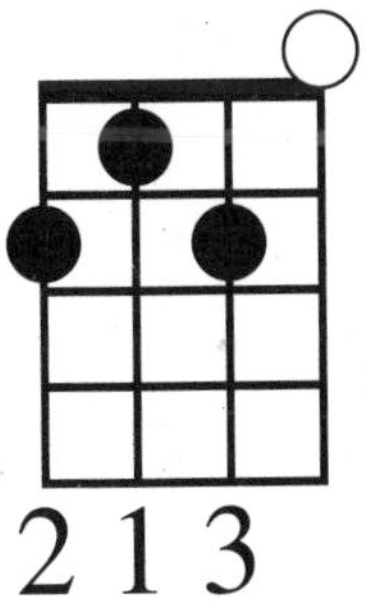

F♯m
4fr.
3 4 2 1

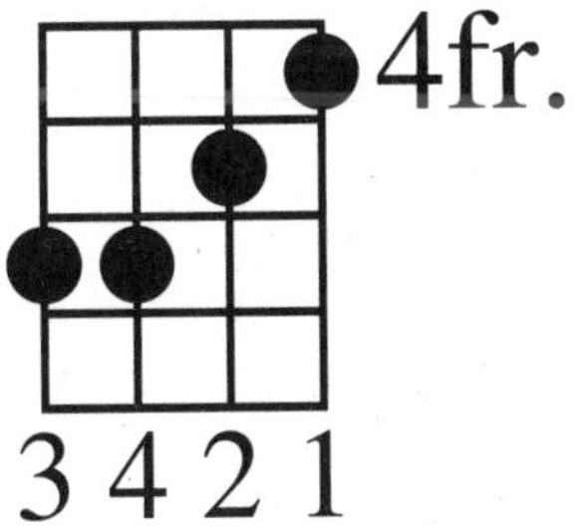

F♯m7
1 3 1 4

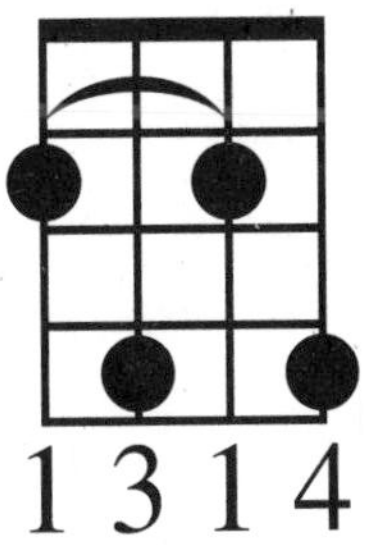

F♯m6
1 2 1 4

F♯7
2 3 1 4

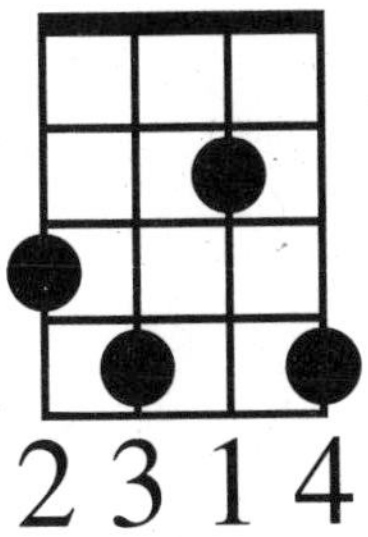

F♯7
4fr.
2 1 3 1

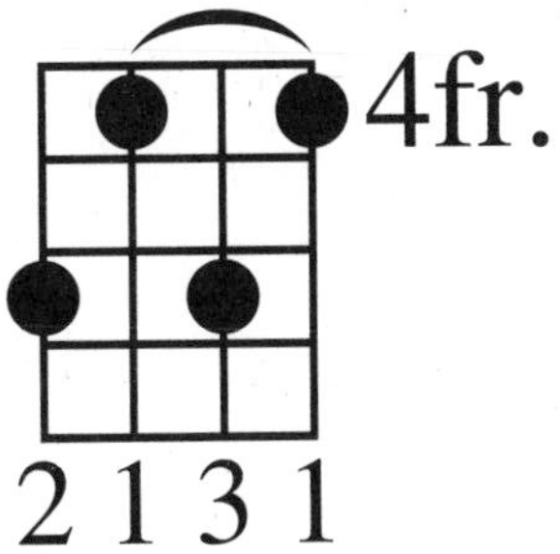

F♯9
1 3 3 3

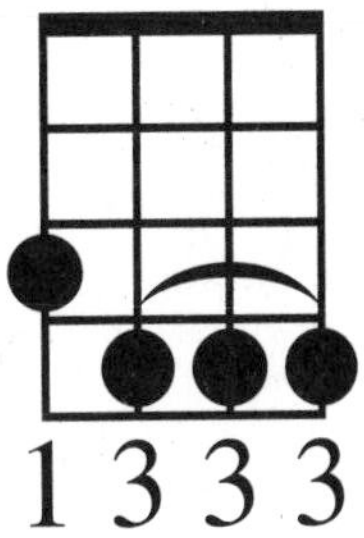

F♯13
3fr.
1 2 2 4

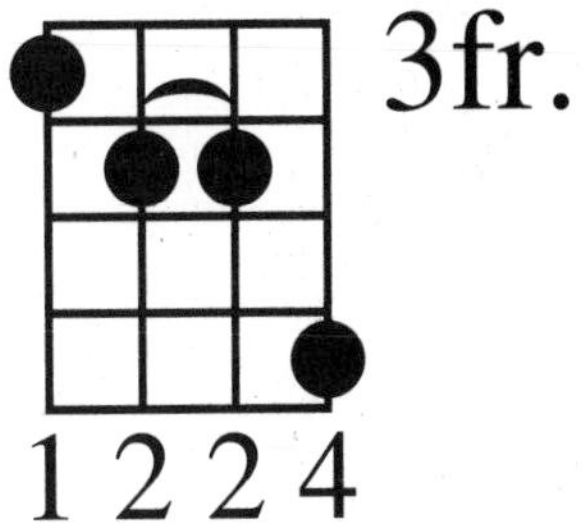

F♯sus
4 1 2

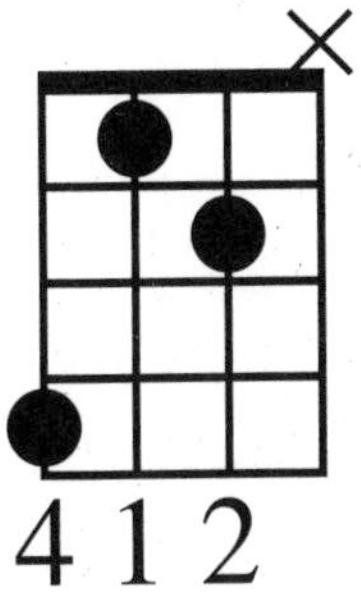

F♯7sus
4fr.
2   3

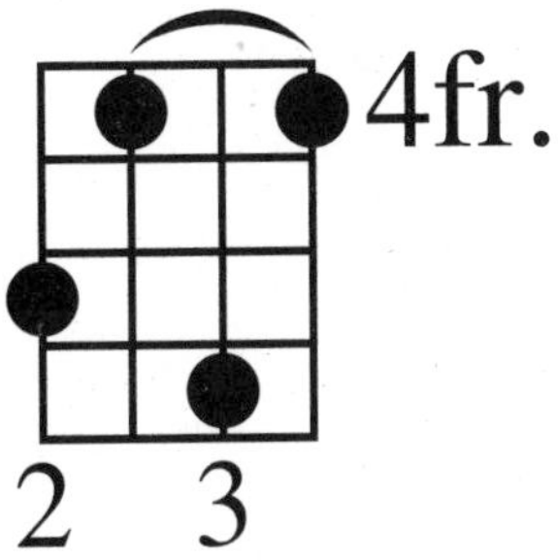

F♯dim7
1 3 2 4

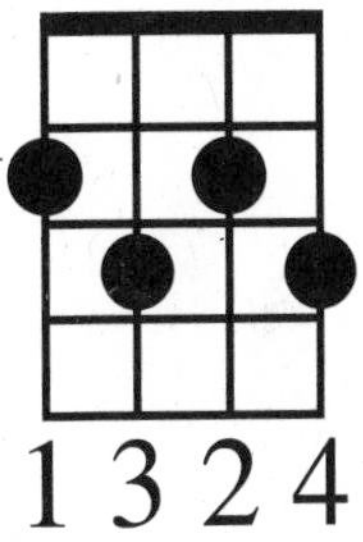

F♯+
4 2 3 1

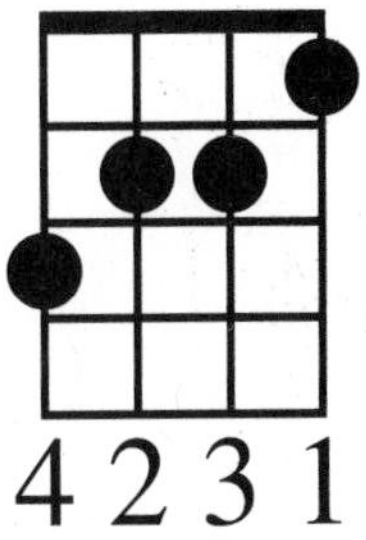

*F♯ and G♭ are two names for the same note.

G CHORDS

G
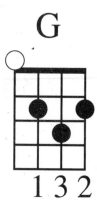
1 3 2

G
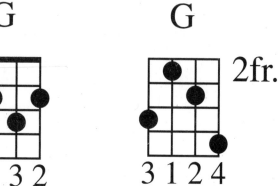
2fr.
3 1 2 4

Gmaj7
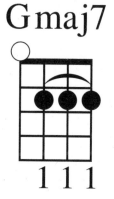
1 1 1

G6
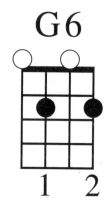
1   2

Gm
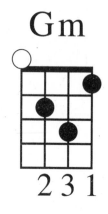
2 3 1

Gm
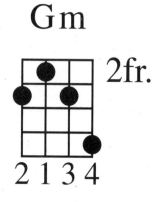
2fr.
2 1 3 4

Gm7
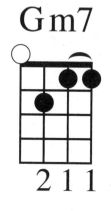
2 1 1

Gm6
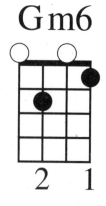
2   1

G7
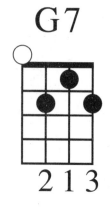
2 1 3

G7
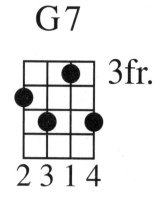
3fr.
2 3 1 4

G9
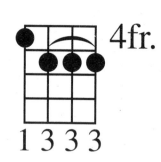
4fr.
1 3 3 3

G13
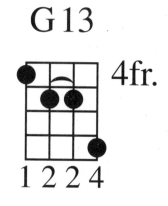
4fr.
1 2 2 4

Gsus

1 2 3

G7sus
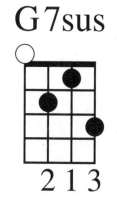
2 1 3

Gdim7
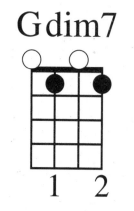
1   2

G+
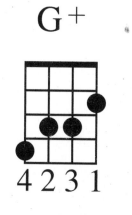
4 2 3 1

A♭ (G♯) CHORDS

A♭
3fr.
3 1 2 1

A♭
3fr.
3 1 2 4

A♭maj7
3fr.
3 1 1 1

A♭6
3fr.
3 4 2 1

A♭m
1 3 4 2

A♭m
3fr.
2 1 3 4

A♭m7
1 4 2 3

A♭m6
1 3 1 2

A♭7
1 3 2 4

A♭7
4fr.
2 3 1 4

A♭9
1 3 2 1

A♭13
5fr.
1 2 2 4

A♭sus
×
1 2 3

A♭7sus
1 3 2 4

A♭dim7
1 3 2 4

A♭+
3fr.
4 2 3 1

*A♭ and G♯ are two names for the same note.

Glossary

accent Emphasis on a beat, note, or chord.

accidental A sharp, flat, or natural sign that occurs in a measure.

altered tuning Any tuning other than standard tuning on the ukulele.

arpeggio The notes of a chord played one after another instead of simultaneously.

backbeats In $\frac{4}{4}$ time, beats 2 and 4 in a measure. In most types of rock and pop music, the drummer usually accents the backbeats by hitting the snare, giving the music a strong feeling of forward momentum.

bar See *measure (or bar)*.

bar line A vertical line that indicates where one measure ends and another begins.

barre To fret multiple strings with one finger.

barre chord A chord played by fretting several strings with one finger.

bridge The part of the ukulele that anchors the strings to the body.

brush stroke To lightly strum the ukulele strings with the index finger of the right hand.

capo A device placed around the neck of the ukulele to raise the pitch of the strings.

chord A group of three or more notes played simultaneously.

chord progression A sequence of chords played in succession.

coda 1: An ending section of a movement or piece. 2: The symbol fi .

common time The most common time signature found in music; there are four beats to every measure and the quarter note gets one beat. Same as $\frac{4}{4}$.

countermelody A melody played at the same time as the main melody.

cut time A time signature that usually indicates a faster tempo where there are two beats to every measure and the half note gets one beat. Same as $\frac{2}{2}$.

dotted note A note followed by a dot, indicating that the length of the note is longer by one half of the note's original length.

double bar line A sign made of one thin line and one thick line, indicating the end of a piece of music.

double stop A group of two notes played simultaneously.

downbeat The first beat of a measure.

down-pick To pick the string downward, toward the floor.

down-stroke   To strike the strings downward, toward the floor.

down-strum   To strum the strings downward, toward the floor.

dyad   Two notes played together.

economy of motion   A concept for efficient playing that involves moving as few fingers as little as possible when changing chords.

eighth note   A note equal to half a quarter note, or one half beat in $\frac{4}{4}$ time.

eighth rest   A rest equal to the duration of an eighth note.

enharmonic   Two notes of the same pitch, but with different names. For example, B♭ and A♯ are enharmonic notes.

fermata   A symbol that indicates to hold a note for about twice as long as usual.

fifth   The 5th note of a scale above the root note, the distance of seven half steps.

fingerboard   See *fretboard*.

flat   A symbol that indicates to lower a note one half step.

fret   The metal strips across the fretboard of a ukulele.

fretboard   The part of the ukulele neck where the frets lay.

G clef   See *treble clef*.

grace note   A small note played quickly either just before a beat or right on the beat.

groove   The sense of rhythm in a piece of music.

half note   A note equal to two quarter notes, or two beats in $\frac{4}{4}$ time.

half rest   A rest equal to the duration of a half note.

half step   The distance of one fret on the ukulele.

hammer-on   A technique by which a note is made to sound after playing the string with the right hand by tapping down on the string with another finger of the fretting hand.

harmony   The result of two or more tones played simultaneously.

interval   The distance in pitch between notes.

key   The tonal center of a piece of music.

key signature   The group of sharps or flats that appears at the beginning of a piece of music to indicate what key the music is in.

ledger lines   Short horizontal lines used to extend a staff either higher or lower.

low G tuning   A variation of standard ukulele tuning in which the strings are tuned (starting from the string closest to the ceiling) G–C–E–A. The difference between the two tunings is that, in Low G, the G string is tuned one octave lower than in standard uke tuning.

major chord   A chord consisting of a root, a major 3rd, and a perfect 5th.

major scale   The most common scale in music, consisting of a specific order of whole and half steps: W–W–H–W–W–W–H.

major third   A note that is four half steps up from the root.

measure (or bar)   Divisions of the staff that are separated by bar lines and contain equal numbers of beats.

minor chord   A chord consisting of a root, a minor 3rd, and a perfect 5th.

minor third   A note that is three half steps up from the root.

mode   A set of notes arranged into a specific scale.

mute   To stop a note from ringing on the ukulele by placing either the right or left hand over the strings.

natural   A symbol that indicates a note is not sharp or flat.

note   A symbol used to represent a musical tone.

nut   The part of the ukulele at the top of the neck that aligns the strings over the fretboard.

octave   The interval between two immediate notes of the same name, equivalent to 12 frets on the ukulele, or eight scale steps.

open G tuning   An altered tuning for the ukulele in which the strings are tuned (starting from the string closest to the ceiling) G–B–D–G.

open position   Fingering for chords that incorporates open strings and no barre.

open tuning   An altered tuning in which the strings are tuned to the notes of a major or minor chord.

palm mute   A technique of muffling the strings with the right hand palm at the bridge of the ukulele.

pendulum strumming   A technique in which you keep your arm moving up and down even if a strum is not indicated. The idea is keep a strong groove by not breaking strumming momentum.

pick   A device used to pluck or strum the strings of a ukulele. Note that picks are rarely used to play the instrument.

pima   Abbreviations for the right hand fingers in fingerpicking notation, in which p = thumb, i = index finger, m = middle finger, and a = ring finger.

pinch technique   A fingerpicking technique in which the right hand plucks two strings at once between the thumb and another finger.

pitch   The location of a note related to its lowness or highness.

position   The location of the hand on the fretboard at a particular fret.

pull-off   A left hand technique in which two notes are fingered on the same string, and the lower note is then made to sound by pulling the fretting finger off the higher note.

quarter note   A note equal to one beat in $\frac{4}{4}$ time and the basic unit of musical time.

quarter rest   A rest equal to the duration of a quarter note.

reentrant tuning   For stringed instruments, a tuning in which the strings are not tuned in order from lowest to highest pitch. Standard tuning on a ukulele is reentrant.

repeat signs   A group of various symbols indicating sections of music to be played over again.

rest   A symbol representing measured silence in music.

rhythm   The musical organization of beats.

riff   A short, repeated melodic pattern.

root note   The fundamental note of a chord, and also the note that gives the chord its letter name. The root is the first note of the corresponding major scale.

scale   A set of notes arranged in a specific order of whole steps and half steps. The most common scale is the major scale.

scratch rhythm   A percussive technique in which strings muted by fret-hand fingers are strummed.

sharp   A symbol that indicates to raise a note one half step.

shuffle rhythm   A rhythm in which eighth notes are played in an uneven, long-short manner.

sixteenth note   A note equal to half an eighth note, or one quarter beat in $\frac{4}{4}$ time.

sixteenth rest   A rest equal to the duration of a sixteenth note.

slash chord   A chord with a note other than the root in the bass. These are labeled with the chord name on the left, followed by a slash with the bass note listed to the right.

slide   1: A technique of moving smoothly from one note to another. A note is fingered by the left hand and played by the right hand, then the left hand finger maintains pressure while sliding quickly on the string to the next note without interrupting the sound or picking again. Indicated in notation with a diagonal line between notes. 2: A metal or glass tubing that fits over a left hand finger, used to fret the strings and produce slide notes.

staccato   To play notes in a short, detached manner. Indicated in notation by a dot directly over or under the note or chord.

staff   The horizontal lines and spaces upon which music notes are placed to designate their pitch.

standard tuning   The normal tuning for the ukulele in which the strings are tuned (starting from the string closest to the ceiling) G–C–E–A.

strum   To play several strings by brushing quickly across them with the fingers or (rarely for ukulele) a pick.

swing   To play eighth notes in an uneven, long-short rhythm.

syncopation   A shift of rhythmic emphasis to the weak beat, or to a weak part of a beat.

TAB   Abbreviation for *tablature*.

tablature   A system of notation that, for ukulele, uses a graphic representation of the four strings of the ukulele with numbers indicating which fret to play.

tempo   The speed at which music is played.

tie   A curved line that joins two or more notes of the same pitch, indicating to play them as one continuous note.

time signature   A sign resembling a fraction that appears at the beginning of a piece of music. The top number indicates how many beats are in each measure and the bottom number indicates what kind of note gets one beat.

treble clef   A symbol at the beginning of the staff that designates the second line as the note G. Also called the *G clef*.

tremolo picking   Quickly picking a single note, dyad, or chord.

triplet   A group of three notes played in the time of two.

unison   The same pitch played at the same time on different strings of the ukulele.

up-pick   To pick the string upward, toward the ceiling.

up-stroke   To strike the strings upward, toward the ceiling.

up-strum   To strum the strings upward, toward the ceiling.

vibrato   A rapid fluctuation of pitch slightly higher or lower than the main pitch, usually achieved by quickly bending a string up and down repeatedly.

whole note   A note equal to four quarter notes, or four beats in $\frac{4}{4}$ time.

whole rest   A rest equal to the duration of a whole note, or the duration of any full measure.

whole step   The distance of two frets on the ukulele.

The following blank chord frames may be used to keep track of new chords. Write them here as you learn so you won't forget them.

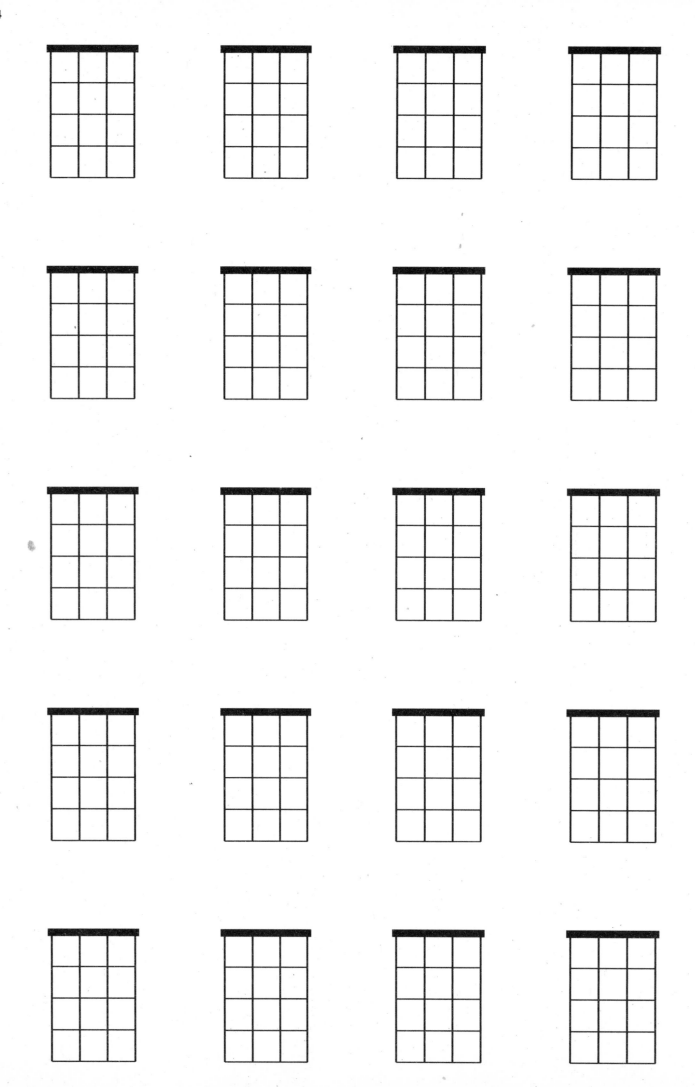